RL: 7.3

8371

342.73
RIT   Ritchie, Donald A.

            The U.S. Consti-
            tution

DUE DATE	BRODART	02/92	14.95

8371

The U.S. Constitution

The U.S. Constitution

Donald A. Ritchie

CHELSEA HOUSE PUBLISHERS

On the Cover: The Preamble and Article 1 of the U.S. Constitution. (Left) Howard Chandler Christy's 1940 painting entitled *Scene at the Signing of the Constitution of the United States.* (Right) A group protests religious discrimination, exercising its constitutional right to peacefully assemble.

Chelsea House Publishers
Editor-in-Chief: Nancy Toff
Executive Editor: Remmel T. Nunn
Managing Editor: Karyn Gullen Browne
Copy Chief: Juliann Barbato
Picture Editor: Adrian G. Allen
Art Director: Maria Epes
Manufacturing Manager: Gerald Levine

Know Your Government
Senior Editor: Kathy Kuhtz

Staff for THE U.S. CONSTITUTION
Associate Editor: Pierre Hauser
Assistant Editor: Gillian Bucky
Copy Editor: Karen Hammonds
Deputy Copy Chief: Ellen Scordato
Editorial Assistant: Theodore Keyes
Picture Researcher: Dixon and Turner Research Associates
Assistant Art Director: Laurie Jewell
Designer: Noreen M. Lamb
Layout: Donna Sinisgalli
Production Coordinator: Joseph Romano

3   5   7   9   8   6   4   2

Library of Congress Cataloging-in-Publication Data

Ritchie, Donald A., 1945–
    The U.S. Constitution / Donald A. Ritchie.
        p.   cm. — (Know your government)
    Bibliography: p.
    Includes index.
    Summary: Surveys the history of the United States Constitution with descriptions of its structure, current function, and influence in our society.
    ISBN 0-87754-894-3
            0-7910-0877-0 (pbk.)
    1. United States—Constitutional history—Juvenile literature. [1. United States—Constitutional history.]   I. Title.   II. Title: US Constitution.   III. Series: Know your government (New York, N.Y.)
KF4541.Z9R58   1988   88–14112
342.73'029—dc19   CIP
[347.30229]   AC

CONTENTS

KNOW YOUR GOVERNMENT

CHELSEA HOUSE PUBLISHERS

INTRODUCTION

Government: Crises of Confidence

Arthur M. Schlesinger, jr.

From the start, Americans have regarded their government with a mixture of reliance and mistrust. The men who founded the republic did not doubt the indispensability of government. "If men were angels," observed the 51st Federalist Paper, "no government would be necessary." But men are not angels. Because human beings are subject to wicked as well as to noble impulses, government was deemed essential to assure freedom and order.

At the same time, the American revolutionaries knew that government could also become a source of injury and oppression. The men who gathered in Philadelphia in 1787 to write the Constitution therefore had two purposes in mind. They wanted to establish a strong central authority and to limit that central authority's capacity to abuse its power.

To prevent the abuse of power, the Founding Fathers wrote two basic principles into the new Constitution. The principle of federalism divided power between the state governments and the central authority. The principle of the separation of powers subdivided the central authority itself into three branches—the executive, the legislative, and the judiciary—so that "each may be a check on the other." The *Know Your Government* series focuses on the major executive departments and agencies in these branches of the federal government.

7

The Constitution did not plan the executive branch in any detail. After vesting the executive power in the president, it assumed the existence of "executive departments" without specifying what these departments should be. Congress began defining their functions in 1789 by creating the Departments of State, Treasury, and War. The secretaries in charge of these departments made up President Washington's first cabinet. Congress also provided for a legal officer, and President Washington soon invited the attorney general, as he was called, to attend cabinet meetings. As need required, Congress created more executive departments.

Setting up the cabinet was only the first step in organizing the American state. With almost no guidance from the Constitution, President Washington, seconded by Alexander Hamilton, his brilliant secretary of the treasury, equipped the infant republic with a working administrative structure. The Federalists believed in both executive energy and executive accountability and set high standards for public appointments. The Jeffersonian opposition had less faith in strong government and preferred local government to the central authority. But when Jefferson himself became president in 1801, although he set out to change the direction of policy, he found no reason to alter the framework the Federalists had erected.

By 1801 there were about 3,000 federal civilian employees in a nation of a little more than 5 million people. Growth in territory and population steadily enlarged national responsibilities. Thirty years later, when Jackson was president, there were more than 11,000 government workers in a nation of 13 million. The federal establishment was increasing at a faster rate than the population.

Jackson's presidency brought significant changes in the federal service. He believed that the executive branch contained too many officials who saw their jobs as "species of property" and as "a means of promoting individual interest." Against the idea of a permanent service based on life tenure, Jackson argued for the periodic redistribution of federal offices, contending that this was the democratic way and that official duties could be made "so plain and simple that men of intelligence may readily qualify themselves for their performance." He called this policy rotation-in-office. His opponents called it the spoils system.

In fact, partisan legend exaggerated the extent of Jackson's removals. More than 80 percent of federal officeholders retained their jobs. Jackson discharged no larger a proportion of government workers than Jefferson had done a generation earlier. But the rise in these years of mass political parties gave federal patronage new importance as a means of building the party and of rewarding activists. Jackson's successors were less restrained in the distribution of spoils. As the federal establishment grew—to nearly 40,000 by 1861—the politicization of the public service excited increasing concern.

After the Civil War the spoils system became a major political issue. High-minded men condemned it as the root of all political evil. The spoilsmen, said the British commentator James Bryce, "have distorted and depraved the mechanism of politics." Patronage, by giving jobs to unqualified, incompetent, and dishonest persons, lowered the standards of public service and nourished corrupt political machines. Office-seekers pursued presidents and cabinet secretaries without mercy. "Patronage," said Ulysses S. Grant after his presidency, "is the bane of the presidential office." "Every time I appoint someone to office," said another political leader, "I make a hundred enemies and one ingrate." George William Curtis, the president of the National Civil Service Reform League, summed up the indictment. He said,

> The theory which perverts public trusts into party spoils, making public
> employment dependent upon personal favor and not on proved merit,
> necessarily ruins the self-respect of public employees, destroys the
> function of party in a republic, prostitutes elections into a desperate
> strife for personal profit, and degrades the national character by lower-
> ing the moral tone and standard of the country.

The object of civil service reform was to promote efficiency and honesty in the public service and to bring about the ethical regeneration of public life. Over bitter opposition from politicians, the reformers in 1883 passed the Pendleton Act, establishing a bipartisan Civil Service Commission, competitive examinations, and appointment on merit. The Pendleton Act also gave the president authority to extend by executive order the number of "classified" jobs—that is, jobs subject to the merit system. The act applied initially only to about 14,000 of the more than 100,000 federal positions. But by the end of the 19th century 40 percent of federal jobs had moved into the classified category.

Civil service reform was in part a response to the growing complexity of American life. As society grew more organized and problems more technical, official duties were no longer so plain and simple that any person of intelligence could perform them. In public service, as in other areas, the all-round man was yielding ground to the expert, the amateur to the professional. The excesses of the spoils system thus provoked the counter-ideal of scientific public administration, separate from politics and, as far as possible, insulated against it.

The cult of the expert, however, had its own excesses. The idea that administration could be divorced from policy was an illusion. And in the realm of policy, the expert, however much segregated from partisan politics, can

9

never attain perfect objectivity. He remains the prisoner of his own set of values. It is these values rather than technical expertise that determine fundamental judgments of public policy. To turn over such judgments to experts, moreover, would be to abandon democracy itself; for in a democracy final decisions must be made by the people and their elected representatives. "The business of the expert," the British political scientist Harold Laski rightly said, "is to be on tap and not on top."

Politics, however, were deeply ingrained in American folkways. This meant intermittent tension between the presidential government, elected every four years by the people, and the permanent government, which saw presidents come and go while it went on forever. Sometimes the permanent government knew better than its political masters; sometimes it opposed or sabotaged valuable new initiatives. In the end a strong president with effective cabinet secretaries could make the permanent government responsive to presidential purpose, but it was often an exasperating struggle.

The struggle within the executive branch was less important, however, than the growing impatience with bureaucracy in society as a whole. The 20th century saw a considerable expansion of the federal establishment. The Great Depression and the New Deal led the national government to take on a variety of new responsibilities. The New Deal extended the federal regulatory apparatus. By 1940, in a nation of 130 million people, the number of federal workers for the first time passed the 1 million mark. The Second World War brought federal civilian employment to 3.8 million in 1945. With peace, the federal establishment declined to around 2 million by 1950. Then growth resumed, reaching 2.8 million by the 1980s.

The New Deal years saw rising criticism of "big government" and "bureaucracy." Businessmen resented federal regulation. Conservatives worried about the impact of paternalistic government on individual self-reliance, on community responsibility, and on economic and personal freedom. The nation in effect renewed the old debate between Hamilton and Jefferson in the early republic, although with an ironic exchange of positions. For the Hamiltonian constituency, the "rich and well-born," once the advocate of affirmative government, now condemned government intervention, while the Jeffersonian constituency, the plain people, once the advocate of a weak central government and of states' rights, now favored government intervention.

In the 1980s, with the presidency of Ronald Reagan, the debate has burst out with unusual intensity. According to conservatives, government intervention abridges liberty, stifles enterprise, and is inefficient, wasteful, and arbitrary. It disturbs the harmony of the self-adjusting market and creates worse troubles than it solves. Get government off our backs, according to the popular cliché, and our problems will solve themselves. When government is necessary, let it be at the local level, close to the people. Above all, stop the inexorable growth of the federal government.

In fact, for all the talk about the "swollen" and "bloated" bureaucracy, the federal establishment has not been growing as inexorably as many Americans seem to believe. In 1949, it consisted of 2.1 million people. Thirty years later, while the country had grown by 70 million, the federal force had grown only by 750,000. Federal workers were a smaller percentage of the population in 1985 than they were in 1955—or in 1940. The federal establishment, in short, has not kept pace with population growth. Moreover, national defense and the postal service account for 60 percent of federal employment.

Why then the widespread idea about the remorseless growth of government? It is partly because in the 1960s the national government assumed new and intrusive functions: affirmative action in civil rights, environmental protection, safety and health in the workplace, community organization, legal aid to the poor. Although this enlargement of the federal regulatory role was accompanied by marked growth in the size of government on all levels, the expansion has taken place primarily in state and local government. Whereas the federal force increased by only 27 percent in the 30 years after 1950, the state and local government force increased by an astonishing 212 percent.

Despite the statistics, the conviction flourishes in some minds that the national government is a steadily growing behemoth swallowing up the liberties of the people. The foes of Washington prefer local government, feeling it is closer to the people and therefore allegedly more responsive to popular needs. Obviously there is a great deal to be said for settling local questions locally. But local government is characteristically the government of the locally powerful. Historically, the way the locally powerless have won their human and constitutional rights has often been through appeal to the national government. The national government has vindicated racial justice against local bigotry, defended the Bill of Rights against local vigilantism, and protected natural resources against local greed. It has civilized industry and secured the rights of labor organizations. Had the states' rights creed prevailed, there would perhaps still be slavery in the United States.

The national authority, far from diminishing the individual, has given most Americans more personal dignity and liberty than ever before. The individual freedoms destroyed by the increase in national authority have been in the main the freedom to deny black Americans their rights as citizens; the freedom to put small children to work in mills and immigrants in sweatshops; the freedom to pay starvation wages, require barbarous working hours, and permit squalid working conditions; the freedom to deceive in the sale of goods and securities; the freedom to pollute the environment—all freedoms that, one supposes, a civilized nation can readily do without.

"Statements are made," said President John F. Kennedy in 1963, "labelling the Federal Government an outsider, an intruder, an adversary. . . . The United States Government is not a stranger or not an enemy. It is the people of fifty states joining in a national effort. . . . Only a great national effort by a great people working together can explore the mysteries of space, harvest the products at the bottom of the ocean, and mobilize the human, natural, and material resources of our lands."

So an old debate continues. However, Americans are of two minds. When pollsters ask large, spacious questions—Do you think government has become too involved in your lives? Do you think government should stop regulating business?—a sizable majority opposes big government. But when asked specific questions about the practical work of government—Do you favor social security? unemployment compensation? Medicare? health and safety standards in factories? environmental protection? government guarantee of jobs for everyone seeking employment? price and wage controls when inflation threatens?—a sizable majority approves of intervention.

In general, Americans do not want less government. What they want is more efficient government. They want government to do a better job. For a time in the 1970s, with Vietnam and Watergate, Americans lost confidence in the national government. In 1964, more than three-quarters of those polled had thought the national government could be trusted to do right most of the time. By 1980 only one-quarter was prepared to offer such trust. But by 1984 trust in the federal government to manage national affairs had climbed back to 45 percent.

Bureaucracy is a term of abuse. But it is impossible to run any large organization, whether public or private, without a bureaucracy's division of labor and hierarchy of authority. And we live in a world of large organizations. Without bureaucracy modern society would collapse. The problem is not to abolish bureaucracy, but to make it flexible, efficient, and capable of innovation.

Two hundred years after the drafting of the Constitution, Americans still regard government with a mixture of reliance and mistrust—a good combination. Mistrust is the best way to keep government reliable. Informed criticism is the means of correcting governmental inefficiency, incompetence, and arbitrariness; that is, of best enabling government to play its essential role. For without government, we cannot attain the goals of the Founding Fathers. Without an understanding of government, we cannot have the informed criticism that makes government do the job right. It is the duty of every American citizen to know our government—which is what this series is all about.

The Old Guard Fife and Drum Corps of the U.S. Army marches past Independence Hall in Philadelphia during the celebration of the bicentennial of the Constitution in 1987.

ONE

"If Men Were Angels"

On September 17, 1987, the United States celebrated the 200th anniversary of its Constitution. Americans take pride in having the world's oldest written Constitution, which has carried our nation through wars, vast territorial expansion, and enormous economic and social change. When the Constitution was adopted, the United States consisted of 13 states along the Atlantic seaboard and had a population of less than 4 million. Two hundred years later there were 50 states, stretching across the continent and into the Pacific, with a population of 250 million. The same years saw a matching growth in the size and responsibilities of the federal government, both at home and abroad, as the United States became a world power.

How instrumental has the Constitution been in affecting these changes? How has this 18th-century document helped carry the United States through the 20th century and toward the future? How has the Constitution met the demands of women and minorities for equal rights and protection? Who is responsible for interpreting what the Constitution means and carrying it into effect? These are some of the issues Americans need to explore in order to understand the Constitution as a living document.

Since the adoption of the Constitution, Americans have been analyzing and arguing over the meanings and intentions of its framers. Because the delegates

James Madison represented the state of Virginia at the Constitutional Convention in 1787. In his Notes of Debates in the Federal Convention, *published posthumously in 1840, Madison provided a detailed account of the strategy and ideas of the Founding Fathers during the making of the Constitution.*

to the Constitutional Convention conducted their business in secret and kept only fragmentary records, no one knows all the reasons why various provisions were included or excluded from the final document. No one can even be sure that the framers wanted their debates and intentions to influence future interpretations and implementations of the Constitution. But Americans study the Constitutional Convention and the document it produced to better understand the reasoning behind it and to appreciate the ways in which it has grown with the times. Ultimately, Americans study the Constitution because it is vitally important for all citizens to know their Constitutional rights and to refuse to surrender them.

The delegates came to the Constitutional Convention with strong values of human freedom and independence and principles of self-government that they wove into the Constitution. They also felt deep antagonism toward autocratic and oppressive government, which they sought to avoid at all costs. Yet no matter how wise, learned, and visionary the framers were, they could not anticipate all future needs of the republic. They wrote a document that checked and balanced power among different branches and set limits on government, while at the same time delegating to it vast responsibilities and giving it license to pass sweeping legislation to fulfill those responsibilities.

Perhaps what made them so successful was their realistic view of human nature. The framers of the Constitution did not share some philosophers' belief in human perfectability. They believed that restraints would be necessary on both the people and their leaders. "If men were angels, no government would be necessary," James Madison wrote in defense of the Constitution. "If angels were to govern men, neither external nor internal controls on government would be necessary. In framing a government which is to be administered by men over men, the great difficulty lies in this: You must first enable the government to control the governed; and in the next place, oblige it to control itself."

It was their success in devising a scheme of government to meet this truth that has enabled Americans to preserve both social order and personal freedom over the past two centuries.

England's King John, seated, applies the royal seal to the Magna Carta in 1215. When he signed the Great Charter, King John agreed to his barons' demands that he not encroach on their feudal rights.

TWO

Origins of the Constitution

The American Revolution ended Britain's control over its 13 American colonies. It left unanswered a great question: How would the American people now be governed? The colonies, founded and largely populated by emigrants from Great Britain, had been part of the British Empire for more than 150 years. During this long association the colonists were subjects of the British monarchs and were governed by the acts of the British Parliament. American colonists grew to expect and demand their full rights as English people.

By 1776, when the Continental Congress proclaimed the Declaration of Independence, leaders of the Revolution drew upon British history to justify opposition to an oppressive government. The earliest restraints that the British placed on their kings' arbitrary power dated back to 1215, when King John signed the Magna Carta (Great Charter). During this time in England, the political and social system that prevailed was known as the feudal system. Under the feudal system, people at all levels of society subordinated themselves to others who were more powerful by pledging under oath—a ritual called the feudal contract—to serve the stronger person in return for protection and material support. King John had angered his feudal barons (those who pledged allegiance to him by providing military service and monetary payments) when he made arbitrary decisions about raising money and disregarded the personal rights of the barons under feudal contract. The barons threatened to make war unless the king granted them a new charter. They marched on London to make good their threat. King John met the barons at Runnymede meadow outside of London and there agreed to the Magna Carta. It promised that no free man would be imprisoned without due process of law and that the king would not attempt to collect taxes above a specified amount without the barons' consent. The Magna Carta stood as the foundation of the idea that English people had rights that even the king must respect.

Two landmarks in British constitutional history were erected during the conflicts between Parliament and the monarchy during the 17th century: the Petition of Rights and the Bill of Rights. In 1629, in a dispute with King Charles I, Parliament made four grievances: that troops should not be stationed in private homes without the consent of homeowners; that no taxes should be imposed without Parliament's consent; that conviction of civilians under martial law (temporary rule by military authorities) in time of peace was illegal; and that no one should be imprisoned without formal and justifiable charges. Charles accepted this Petition of Rights in return for Parliament's promise to provide the funds he needed for foreign wars. Sixty years later, in 1689, King James II was overthrown in Britain's Glorious Revolution and William and Mary took the throne. The new monarchs accepted a Bill of Rights, by which they agreed that only Parliament could authorize taxes and raise a standing army (a permanent army of paid soldiers) in peacetime. The Bill of Rights provided that Parliament should be freely elected and convene often; that members of Parliament should have freedom of speech; and that the king could not disobey acts of Parliament.

Added to this heritage, the American colonists had their own history of colonial charters and compacts, or agreements, that established their various forms of self-government. Some colonies began as business ventures and their governments operated under the terms of their company charters. Colonists who were stockholders in the company selected the government councils and helped to pass laws. As early as 1619, Virginia colonists established a legislature, known as the House of Burgesses, whose elected legislators shared authority with the governor. The following year the Pilgrims sailed for Massachusetts seeking religious freedom. Before landing they adopted the Mayflower Compact, in which each person pledged to be bound by the laws that the community would make. When the settlers created new towns and formed new churches, they made "covenants" by which they agreed to live and work together. Whether business or religious, these charters and covenants were forms of contractual agreements whereby individuals established their rights and recognized their obligations through their governments.

The colonists also observed that the Indian tribes of the Iroquois Confederacy, located in present-day New York, possessed an oral constitution, the Great Law of Peace, which governed five Iroquois tribes that had come together to form a league. Also known as the Five Nations, which included the Mohawk, Oneida, Onondaga, Cayuga, and Seneca tribes (a sixth tribe, the Tuscarora, joined the league in 1722), the Confederacy was formed to bring peace to the warring tribes and establish universal peace based on a government of law. Each tribe in the league was permitted to govern itself, but

The Pilgrims sign the Mayflower Compact aboard the **Mayflower** *on November 11, 1620, while anchored in the harbor of Cape Cod. An important model for the Constitution, the compact established that the Pilgrims would be governed by the will of the majority until permanent provisions could be created for their colony.*

Boston colonists abduct one of King George III's tax collectors and prepare to tar and feather him. The colonists objected to taxation without representation in Parliament, rebelled, and declared their independence from England in 1776.

the larger concerns, such as dealings with other tribes and matters of war, were to be decided by the Great Council of Fifty, composed of 50 chiefs from the member tribes. The problems raised during council meetings were discussed, each member was given a chance to speak, and council decisions were based on a consensus. The colonists who negotiated treaties with the Indians learned about their rules of order. George Washington, James Madison, and Benjamin Franklin all served as colonial negotiators of treaties with the Iroquois. In his Albany Plan of Union, Franklin urged the colonists to adopt a government modeled on the Iroquois' federation, which promoted the equal rights of all the tribes.

Because of their distance from London and the vast amount of land available for both geographic and social mobility, the American colonists possessed even greater freedom than did the people of Britain. Americans became accustomed to the idea of representative government through the election of colonial legislatures. Their local legislatures affected their lives more directly than did

22

the British Parliament, which was largely distracted by wars and European politics. In the mid-18th century, Parliament turned its attention to its colonies and tried to establish more efficient rule—and to collect new revenue. Dissension began when Parliament enacted the Stamp Act (1765) and the Townshend Acts (1767). The Stamp Act provided for revenue stamps to be attached to all newspapers, pamphlets, and business documents such as licenses, commercial bills, notes and bonds, legal documents, and advertisements. The revenue was to be used in the colonies for protecting and securing the colonies by the British. The Townshend Acts laid duties on numerous imports into the colonies, including paint, lead, paper, and tea. The purpose of this money was to pay the salaries of royal governors and judges, thereby rendering them independent of the colonial legislatures. The colonists objected to what they saw as infringements of their traditional rights. Because they could elect no members of Parliament and Parliament was taxing them, they protested against taxation without representation. Parliament passed even stiffer measures to coerce the colonists into cooperation. The "Intolerable Acts" of 1773 closed the port of Boston and placed Massachusetts under the control of a military commander, quartered troops in Boston homes, and threatened those suspected of a major crime with transportation to Britain for trial in English courts. But these actions only pushed the Americans into open rebellion.

Rebelling against Britain was no easy decision for the American colonists. Many of them remained loyal to the king and Parliament. Others showed indifference to both sides in the political struggle. Probably only a minority of the colonists supported the Revolution. Those who led the Revolution therefore felt the need to justify their actions, to explain themselves, to win over undecided colonists, and to gain support from the world.

The leaders of the Revolution were learned men who had studied the classical republics of Greece and Rome, as well as the ideas of the Italian Renaissance (c.1420–1527), the Protestant Reformation (c.1517–1648), and the Enlightenment (c.1690–1770). They especially cited the philosophers of the Enlightenment (a movement in Europe that was marked by a rejection of traditional social, religious, and political ideas and emphasized instead reliance on reason and experience), who believed in natural law and natural rights: that unchangeable laws govern the political world just as surely as they do the physical world. Nations that obeyed these natural laws would find happiness and prosperity; those that did not would fall on hard times.

The writers that the Americans most frequently quoted in defense of their rights were John Locke, Baron de Montesquieu, and Sir William Blackstone.

John Locke, a 17th-century English philosopher whose writings were frequently quoted by the Founding Fathers, wrote that the people of a country were endowed with natural rights that could not be abused by government; if government violated the people's rights, it was their duty to abolish that government.

Locke, who wrote at the time of England's Glorious Revolution (1688–89), argued that the king's power came not from God but from the consent of the free people of the land, who were endowed with unalienable rights—natural rights that could not be transferred to another—to life, liberty, and property. People entered into an agreement with their leaders to govern as long as they ruled justly for the common good. If a government became corrupt and violated this agreement, then people had cause for overthrowing it in order to preserve their rights. Locke's *Two Treatises on Government* (1690) served as a handbook for Americans in launching their new nation.

Montesquieu's *The Spirit of the Laws* (1748) further impressed upon American leaders the need for separation of government powers and a system of checks and balances. The French philosopher drew from examples in the British government to reason that only the separation of the functions of government—kings (executive), commons (legislative), and lords (judicial)—would preserve the liberty of the people, by preventing any part of the government from acting despotically. In other words, the powers and functions of government should be divided equally.

Because so many of the revolutionary-era American leaders were lawyers, they were also familiar with Blackstone's four-volume *Commentaries on the Laws of England* (1765–69). Instead of a written constitution, England has a series of charters, declarations, laws, precedents, and court rulings that protect the rights of its subjects. Many of these laws, collectively called common law, originated in the Middle Ages in the decisions of the local courts that applied custom and reason to everyday disputes. Blackstone's *Commentaries* demonstrated how this common law, together with the laws of Parliament, helped restrain British monarchs from exerting arbitrary power. Although American courts often based their decisions on English common law, even after the Revolution, the new nation's citizens also wanted written constitutions to establish limits on their state and national governments.

When Americans took the ideas of the European Enlightenment and applied them to their own situation, they created something uniquely American. Most significantly, social rank and distinction had never been as strongly established in America as in Europe. American revolutionaries such as Thomas Jefferson rejected European notions that governments operated primarily to support the privileged classes. Jefferson insisted that all people had rights and should be allowed to pursue their own self-interest. Thus the concept of equality of opportunity became an important theme of the American republic and of those who later followed Jefferson's ideas (and who called themselves Democratic-Republicans).

On July 4, 1776, the Declaration of Independence echoed the arguments of Locke and other Enlightenment philosophers. In the Declaration's eloquent preamble, Jefferson wrote: "We hold these truths to be self-evident, that all men are created equal, that they are endowed by their Creator with certain unalienable Rights, that among these are Life, Liberty, and the pursuit of Happiness." It was to secure these rights that governments were created, "deriving their just powers from the consent of the governed." Because the established government had become destructive of these ends, "it is the Right of the People to alter or to abolish it, and to institute new Government." Significantly, the Declaration did not base its demands on the "rights of

Members of the Continental Congress sign the Declaration of Independence on July 4, 1776. The Declaration was created to announce the birth of a new nation and to express the political and social principles upon which the Revolution rested.

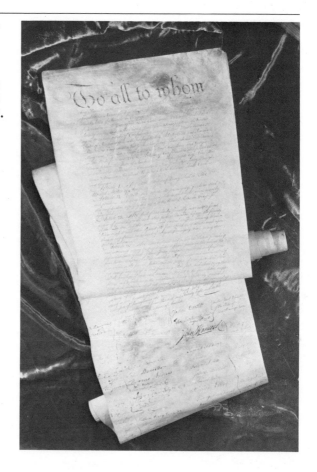

The Articles of Confederation, the precursor of the Constitution, were drafted by Congress in 1777 and ratified by the states in 1781. The Articles established the first national government, consisting of a single legislative body in which each state had one vote.

Englishmen," but upon the universal rights of all people. It became a model for human freedom and independence around the world.

Eight years of warfare and sacrifice followed before a peace treaty was signed, through which Great Britain recognized America's independence. During that time, Americans moved to "institute new Government." The Continental Congress that issued the Declaration of Independence had been created to meet the immediate emergency of the Revolution, but Americans wanted a more formal national government. In 1777, Congress presented the Articles of Confederation to the states. Not until 1781 did the 13th state, Maryland, ratify the Articles and enable them to go into effect.

Having thrown off one strong government, Americans were hardly anxious to embrace another. The first national government under the Articles of

Confederation consisted only of a loose association of 13 states. The states retained the real powers of government. During the Revolution, the states had written their own constitutions. These state constitutions had certain common threads: In defense against potential tyranny, they listed the rights of citizens that government could not violate, such as freedom of the press and trial by jury. They emphasized that government power came from the people and that state offices were to be elected, not hereditary (inherited) positions. The primary form of state government was legislative and the state constitutions gave governors only limited powers. Some states, such as Pennsylvania, created only a one-house legislature—believing that there should be no "House of Lords" in America. (The British Parliament is divided into the House of Lords, whose members are hereditary nobles, and the House of Commons, whose members are elected by the people.) However, most states thought that an upper house of legislature was necessary to represent property owners and to place a check on the poorer classes.

The national government under the Articles of Confederation consisted of a single legislative body, with no executive or judiciary. All government affairs were handled by congressional committees. Every state, no matter what the size of its population, had just one vote in Congress. The Congress could raise money only by asking the states for it; Congress had no means to force a state to pay its share. Several states, indeed, did not pay their share of the government's financial support. Once, in 1783, Congress had to flee when American soldiers marched on the capital in Philadelphia to demand their back pay. The credit of the new nation was weak because it had not paid its war debts, largely because the states disagreed on how to proceed. This discouraged both foreign and domestic investments in the new nation and made it difficult to raise money to fund government operations. The government under the Articles could claim some major achievements, most notably the Northwest Ordinance (1787), which organized the Western territories. But it was usually difficult to get 13 independent states to work together.

Alexander Hamilton, a New York delegate to the Continental Congress who had been George Washington's aide during the American Revolution, dismissed the Articles as merely the "appearance" of a Union. He saw the nation as really 13 "jarring, jealous" states, unhappy at home and weak in the eyes of the world. George Washington and other revolutionary war leaders feared that they had achieved a nation without a national government. They saw the nation's many commercial, financial, social, and diplomatic problems as essentially political in nature and believed that the only solution was a stronger, more effective central government. As Washington wrote, "I predict the worst consequences from a half-starved, limping government, always moving upon crutches and tottering at every step."

In 1785, the states of Virginia and Maryland sent delegates to a meeting to settle differences over navigation rights on the Potomac River, which separated them. When Maryland's delegates reached Alexandria, Virginia, they found that Virginia's delegates had not yet arrived. Anxious that the meeting succeed, George Washington graciously invited all the delegates to his nearby estate, Mount Vernon. At the Mount Vernon Conference the delegates discussed tolls and fishing rights on the Potomac River and raised issues that went beyond the boundaries and the authority of the two states involved. James Madison, who headed the committee in Virginia's assembly that received the conference's report, concluded that the national government

George Washington greets a visitor to his Virginia home, Mount Vernon. Washington invited Virginia and Maryland delegates to a conference at Mount Vernon in 1785 to settle a boundary dispute that involved navigation rights on the Potomac River.

Massachusetts farmers encourage a supporter of Shays's Rebellion as he fights an opponent. In 1786, a mob of desperate farmers, led by Daniel Shays, rebelled against the state courts when the courts allowed creditors to foreclose on mortgages to collect debts.

needed to address such questions as commerce between the states. Madison persuaded the Virginia Assembly to pass a resolution calling for a convention of the states to deal with interstate commerce. That convention met in Annapolis, Maryland, in the fall of 1786—but only six states sent representatives. There Virginia's James Madison and New York's Alexander Hamilton persuaded other delegates that more than questions of commerce were involved. They called for a convention to meet the next year in Philadelphia to consider a constitution for a federal government that would be sufficiently strong to meet the needs of the Union.

For those who doubted the urgency of overhauling the central government, events in Massachusetts that winter shocked them into action. Farmers in western Massachusetts had been hard hit by falling prices, higher taxes, and increased farm foreclosures (repossession of property by a creditor to whom money is owed). Led by Daniel Shays, a veteran of the revolutionary war, the farmers banded together, shut down the state courts to stop creditors from collecting their debts, halted sheriffs' auctions of farm lands, and attacked the federal arsenal at Springfield. When Massachusetts pleaded with Congress for aid, Congress was unable to help because it had neither an adequate army nor money. The Massachusetts militia easily defeated Shays's rebellion, but the national government had shown itself powerless to defend itself against such internal violence. The rebellion struck terror in the wealthier people of the states, who feared a general assault on property. Men such as George Washington considered the experience humiliating for America. John Hancock, governor of Massachusetts, believed that it demonstrated that America's future depended on strengthening the union between the states.

Congress reluctantly authorized a convention, although it did not specify what sort of a meeting or how broad its objectives were. Twelve state legislatures (Rhode Island had declined the invitation to participate) chose delegates "to remedy the defects in our federal Union," as New Hampshire's resolution declared. The stage was set for the creation of a new government.

Independence Hall in Philadelphia, Pennsylvania. The 55 delegates to the Constitutional Convention met here during the summer of 1787 to plan a new federal government.

THREE

The Constitutional Convention

Fifty-five delegates gathered in Philadelphia during the summer of 1787. There they met in Independence Hall, in the same chamber where 11 years earlier the Declaration of Independence had been signed. The Declaration had proclaimed America free from British rule, but the new Federal Convention faced the even greater task of building a strong and effective national government. Not everyone wanted sweeping change. Nineteen delegates did not bother to attend and one of the states, Rhode Island, sent no delegates at all. Among those who attended there were considerable differences of opinion about what should be done.

For the most part the delegates were wealthy, well-educated property owners. Some were lawyers from the cities; others were planters from the countryside. George Washington, who had commanded the American armies during the Revolution, lent his personal prestige to the convention. Other delegates had fought under Washington in the revolutionary war and now wanted a central government to preserve and extend the rights and liberties they had won on the battlefield. Eight of them had signed their names to the Declaration of Independence. Forty-two had served in the Congress of the United States and most of the rest had served in state government. Many had experience drafting their state constitutions.

Despite their extensive experience, the delegates were still relatively young. Their average age was 46, with Jonathan Dayton of New Jersey the youngest at 26, and Benjamin Franklin the oldest at 81. In many ways they represented the best minds in America. Thomas Jefferson, who was absent from the convention because he was serving as American minister to France, looked over the list of delegates and commented, "It really is an assembly of demigods."

The most important delegate was the small, scholarly young representative from Virginia, James Madison. Madison had studied at the College of New Jersey (later named Princeton University) and had served in the Virginia legislature and in Congress. A diligent student of the ancient governments of Greece and Rome and of political theory, Madison came to Philadelphia well prepared with a plan for a stronger central government. Under his plan the larger states would have greater representation than the smaller ones, the central government would have authority over the states, and a national judiciary would be superior to state courts. "Every person seems to acknowledge his greatness," another delegate said of Madison. "He blends together the profound politician with the scholar."

The delegates decided that they must debate in absolute secrecy. They promised not to speak about or publish anything on their debates without permission and barred the doors and windows to prevent any news from leaking out. Madison later insisted that "no Constitution would ever have been adopted by the convention if the debates had been public." Secrecy kept the state legislatures from interfering in their deliberations and permitted the delegates some flexibility in their positions—they could change their minds without public censure.

Secrecy ensured that there *was* a debate. Members rose to make both long and short speeches, to question each other, and to rebut differing opinions. They tried to convince one another by logic, humor, passion, and some threats. Some may have occasionally exaggerated their speeches to create an effect. Because of their concern for secrecy, they did not leave future generations an exact record of what they said, but James Madison took a front seat where he could hear everything, and he took extensive notes on the debates. Today, most of our knowledge of what the convention did, and the reasons behind the delegates' actions, comes from Madison's notes.

At the beginning of the convention, on May 29, Virginia's Governor Edmund Randolph addressed the delegates about the grave weakness in the structure of government under the Articles of Confederation. Randolph placed before

34

Edmund Randolph, governor of Virginia and a delegate to the Constitutional Convention, presented the Virginia Plan. The plan provided for executive and judicial branches and a two-house legislature, with members of both houses apportioned according to population.

them a plan designed to promote "peace, harmony, happiness, and liberty." The "Virginia Plan" (really the work of James Madison) envisioned a two-house national legislature representing the states on the basis of population, the laws of which would be supreme over the laws of the states. Unlike the current government, the Virginia Plan provided for a president and a judicial branch to

George Washington was appointed presiding officer of the Constitutional Convention, lending prestige to the proceedings, but he made few direct comments during the debates.

balance the Congress. It also included an easier means of amending the Constitution than existed under the Articles, which required the unanimous vote of all the states. Thus the Virginia Plan was a complete rejection of the government under the Articles of Confederation.

The Virginia Plan, based on population, favored the larger states. On June 15, William Paterson of New Jersey presented the plan of the smaller states. The "New Jersey Plan" was really a series of amendments designed to strengthen the current Articles. Its supporters worried that the Virginia Plan went too far in creating a central government and would weaken too much the power of the individual states. The smaller states also feared becoming dominated by the larger states. However, the delegates rejected the New Jersey Plan and committed themselves to creating a new form of government.

The smaller states lost their first battle, but they had enough votes to keep the convention from succeeding, unless their rights were protected under the new government. Eventually, the convention became deadlocked and the delegates were unable to resolve differences between large and small states. To break the impasse, Benjamin Franklin proposed that the delegates "implore the assistance of Heaven" by inviting local ministers to open the convention sessions with prayers. This suggestion was not adopted.

When the convention recessed to celebrate the fourth of July, the delegates appointed a special committee to solve the dispute. To Madison's dismay, the committee compromised on his plan for representation by population. It decided that whereas one house should be apportioned by population, another should have equal representation for all states. As William Samuel Johnson of Connecticut explained, the two houses of Congress were "halves of a unique whole." In one house the people would be represented, in the other the states. Because this proposal was strongly advocated by the Connecticut delegation, it became known as the Connecticut Compromise—or as the Great Compromise, because it saved the Constitution.

Another high hurdle that loomed ahead of the delegates was the "peculiar institution" of slavery. There were 650,000 black slaves in America, nine-tenths of whom lived in southern states. Many people in both the North and South considered slavery morally wrong and believed that it must be ended. Virginia delegate George Mason, himself a slave owner, warned the convention that "every master of slaves is born a petty tyrant. They [slaves and slave owners] bring the judgment of heaven upon a country." But other southern delegates stressed that they would never agree to a Constitution that interfered with their right to own slaves as property.

In this drawing Alexander Hamilton (far left), James Wilson, James Madison (standing), and Benjamin Franklin are shown drafting the Constitution in Franklin's garden.

The Constitution never mentioned slaves or slavery and referred only to "other persons." But the delegates agreed to two important compromises on slavery. They would count three-fifths of the slaves for purposes of taxation and representation in Congress. And the new government would have no power to end the importation of slaves until 1808. Oliver Ellsworth of Connecticut warned that unless such a compromise was accepted the states would separate from each other and bloodshed would follow. He further argued that slavery would not last forever and predicted that "slavery in time will not be a speck in our country."

Another problem concerned how to admit new states into the Union. Some delegates feared that the new western states would someday overwhelm the original 13. However, Roger Sherman of Connecticut pointed out that "we are providing for our posterity, for our children and our grandchildren, who would be as likely to be citizens of new western states, as of the old states." Accepting his reasoning, the convention agreed to admit all new states on an equal basis with the old.

The most dramatic departure from the previous form of government was the creation of an executive branch headed by a president of the United States. Having overthrown rule by a king, many Americans were suspicious of establishing a new monarch. Here the convention benefited from the daily presence of its presiding officer. As one delegate, Pierce Butler of South Carolina, later commented, the powers of the president might not have been so great "had not many of the members cast their eyes towards General

On September 17, 1787, 39 of the 55 delegates to the Constitutional Convention sign the Constitution after they voted to defeat Edmund Randolph's motion to include a bill of rights in the document. Most of the delegates at the convention believed that such rights were already guaranteed by the state constitutions.

Washington as President; and shaped their ideas of the powers to be given a President, by their opinions of his virtue."

When they had finished debating the details of the Constitution, the convention appointed a committee on style to apply the finishing touches. The pen of Gouverneur Morris of Pennsylvania gave the Constitution its final polish. The committee's most important contribution was to change the preamble from "We the People of the States"—listing the 13 states—to simply "We the People of the United States." This phrase made clear that the people, not the states, would be the source of authority of the new national government.

Just as they were finishing their work, several delegates called for a bill of rights in the Constitution. Edmund Randolph warned that he would not be able to sign the document without it. George Mason and Elbridge Gerry also spoke out in support of an explicit protection of the rights of citizens, such as freedom of speech, the press, and religion. However, most delegates believed that a bill

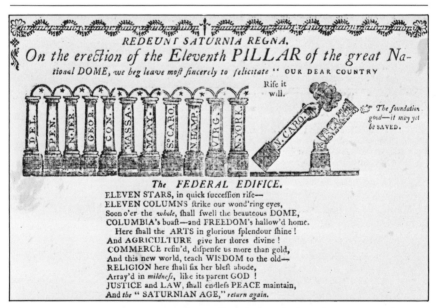

The Federal Pillars, *an engraving that appeared in* The Massachusetts Centinel *on August 2, 1788. To mark each state's ratification of the Constitution, the newspaper published a small allegorical illustration—an upright column inscribed with the state's name—and the prediction "The foundation good—it may yet be saved."*

Alexander Hamilton, a New York delegate to the Constitutional Convention, strongly urged New York to ratify the document. Hamilton, James Madison, and John Jay wrote a series of essays offering reasons for adopting the new federal government.

of rights was unnecessary because such rights were already protected by the state constitutions. The dissenters responded that the new federal government would be supreme over the states and their individual bills of rights. But by now the delegates were too tired and restless to extend the debate. They overwhelmingly defeated Randolph's motion and adopted the Constitution.

The delegates reassembled for the last time on September 17, 1787, to sign the Constitution. The aged Benjamin Franklin urged each member to "doubt a little of his own infallibility" and to join in a unanimous gesture by signing the

41

document. However, only 39 of the 55 delegates signed. Randolph, Mason, and Gerry refused and several others had already left the convention.

As the delegates came forward to pen their names to the Constitution, Franklin looked toward the president's chair, on which a rising sun was painted. He observed that often during the proceedings he looked at it without being sure whether it was rising or setting, "but now at length I have the happiness to know that it is a rising and not a setting sun."

The delegates had proved themselves statesmen. But their work was not over. Now they left for home to convince their states to ratify their handiwork. The Constitution they had drafted would be submitted to conventions in each state for ratification. Realizing that the state legislatures would be reluctant to give up any power, the Constitutional Convention had recommended state conventions as the best way to win approval of the new national government.

The smaller states believed that they had achieved much of what they wanted and speedily ratified the Constitution. Delaware acted first, followed by New Jersey, Connecticut, and Georgia. But in the larger states—Pennsylvania, Massachusetts, Virginia, and New York—there was strong resistance to the new plan still to be overcome.

Because those who favored the Constitution called themselves "Federalists," the opposition became known as "Anti-Federalists." Both names were misleading. The Federalists had created a much stronger national government than had ever existed in America, but their name emphasized federalism, or the union but not consolidation of states. The Anti-Federalists believed in the type of federalism represented by the Articles of Confederation and exemplified by the American political philosopher and writer Thomas Paine's pronouncement, "That government is best which governs least." Still, the Anti-Federalists took an essentially negative position. They opposed the Constitution without offering their own solutions to the problems the Constitution was designed to solve.

Anti-Federalists such as Virginia's Patrick Henry objected that the Constitution threatened the liberties secured during the American Revolution. He objected to the absence of a bill of rights, to the creation of a kinglike president, and to the aristocratic nature of the Senate (senators were to be elected by state legislatures, not by the people). Henry had been chosen as a delegate to the convention, but declined to serve because he said he "smelt a rat." Now he used all of his oratorical eloquence and power to persuade Virginia not to go along with the new national government. The Federalists finally won Virginia's ratification by promising to support a bill of rights in the form of amendments to the Constitution to be passed as soon as possible.

Anti-Federalists were also a strong force at the New York ratifying convention. To explain and defend the Constitution during the New York debate, Federalists Alexander Hamilton, James Madison, and John Jay wrote a series of newspaper essays, which they signed "Publius." These essays, later reprinted as *The Federalist Papers,* provided brilliant analyses of the weaknesses of the Articles of Confederation and the strengths of the proposed government. Not only did they help to sway New York, but they continue today to offer insights into the intentions of the framers of the Constitution. On July 26, 1788, the New York convention voted 30 to 27 in favor of ratification. With 11 states approving, the Constitution had been adopted. Later, North Carolina (in 1789) and Rhode Island (in 1790) followed suit and the last of the 13 states entered the Union. In the fall of 1788, elections were held throughout the states and the new government under the Constitution was launched on March 4, 1789. " 'Tis done," rejoiced one Federalist. "We have become a nation."

The U.S. Capitol, west facade, in Washington, D.C. The Capitol building houses the two branches of the legislature: the House of Representatives and the Senate.

FOUR

The Character of the Constitution

W e the people of the United States," begins the preamble to the Constitution. In these few words the framers made it clear that the new government derived its power not from the states but from the people of the states. Unlike the Declaration of Independence, the Constitution referred to "people" rather than "men." Nor did the Constitution mention God or religion, except to prohibit religious tests for holding federal office. Freedom of religion was added to the Constitution in the first amendment.

The purpose of the Constitution is "to form a more perfect Union," the preamble continues, and to "establish justice, insure domestic tranquility, provide for the common defense, promote the general welfare, and secure the blessings of liberty to ourselves and to our posterity."

Article 1: The Congress

The first three articles of the Constitution established the legislative, executive, and judicial branches of the new federal government. The Constitution deliberately separated the powers of the government among these three independent branches. It established a system of checks and balances, giving each branch some authority to restrain the others. At times this system of divided government has led to inefficiency and to conflict between the president, Congress, and the courts. However, this was the price that the framers believed necessary to pay to prevent any branch from assuming too much power and becoming autocratic.

Under the Articles of Confederation, the government had consisted entirely of a single-body legislature. Article 1 gives all legislative power to a bicameral, or two-house, legislature, which consists of the Senate and House of Representatives. As decided by the Great Compromise, every state has two senators. (This is the only part of the Constitution that cannot be amended because Article 5 provides that "no state, without its consent, shall be deprived of its equal suffrage [vote] in the Senate.") As stated in the provisions of the Constitution, senators were originally elected by the state legislatures; however, after the Seventeenth Amendment was ratified in 1913, this procedure was changed and senators were thereafter elected directly by the people. Senators serve six-year terms and are divided into three classes, so that only one-third of the senators run in each Congressional election. Members of the House have always been elected directly by the people in their districts and fill two-year terms. The entire House stands for election every two years. There are now 100 senators, 435 representatives, and 5 nonvoting delegates from American Samoa, the District of Columbia, Guam, Puerto Rico, and the Virgin Islands.

The Constitution requires that a representative be at least 25 years old and have been a citizen for 7 years at the time of his or her election. Members of the Senate, which the framers expected to be a more senior body, must be 30 years old and have been a citizen for 9 years. The House elects one of its members to be Speaker, or presiding officer; the vice-president serves as the presiding officer of the Senate. The Senate may elect a president pro tempore (temporary) to preside in the vice-president's absence. Otherwise, the Constitution leaves it to the Senate and the House to determine the qualifications of their members and to judge whether their elections are fair or not. The two bodies also have exclusive control over their own "housekeeping": to elect other officers (such as majority and minority party leaders), to set their own rules, and to punish or expel members for unacceptable behavior.

Having met in secret themselves, the framers of the Constitution did not require the new Congress to open its debates to the public. Instead what they stipulated was that each house should keep and publish a journal of its proceedings. These journals consist of short minutes of the debate and tallies of the votes. They do not contain the full text of speeches. Today, Congressional speeches are published in the *Congressional Record*, a daily volume that evolved in later years. Because members of the House were elected by the people and ran for reelection every two years, they immediately decided to open their galleries to public visitors and to the press. By contrast, the first senators thought they could deliberate more calmly and could more freely offer their advice and consent to the president if they were not on public display. From 1789 until 1794, the Senate held all of its meetings in secret. Even after its doors opened to the public in 1794 for legislative sessions, the Senate continued to conduct secret debates on executive business (treaties and nominations). Secret sessions lasted until 1929 and were abandoned only after senators conceded that newspapers were routinely publishing their supposedly secret debates.

The Senate and House must meet at least once a year and neither house may adjourn for more than three days without the consent of the other. The two houses work separately on legislation, but both must agree on a bill before they can send it to the president for his signature. The House and Senate have equal powers in all but three cases: the House alone originates all bills for raising revenue (taxes and tariffs); the Senate alone approves treaties and confirms presidential nominations (for example, when the president nominates a candidate to fill a vacancy on the Supreme Court). These latter provisions made the Senate more influential than the House in foreign affairs, because it had a voice in treaties and diplomatic nominations. But after World War II the vast American expenditures for foreign aid and defense gave the House more influence in foreign affairs, because its support was necessary to appropriate any funds.

Congress, the subject of the first and longest Article of the Constitution, has been called the "first branch" of the federal government. The Constitution gives Congress power to establish and collect taxes, to borrow money, and to coin money. Congress appropriates all the money that the government needs to operate (known as the "power of the purse") and regulates commerce with foreign nations, the states, and Indian tribes. Congress has the power to declare war and to provide for the common defense by raising and supporting armies and navies, to organize the National Guard, and to call out the state militia to suppress insurrections and repel invasions. In addition, Congress has authority to establish post offices and post roads, to establish laws on immigration and naturalization, and to promote the arts and sciences by providing for authors to copyright their books and inventors to patent their inventions.

47

To carry out these obligations, Article 1, section 8 gives the Congress power "to make all laws which shall be necessary and proper." Because this provision gives Congress vast power to write laws on almost every issue, it is known as the "elastic clause."

But Congressional power is not unlimited. Article 1 also prohibits Congress from passing laws on certain issues. Congress could not stop the slave trade until 1808. It could not suspend *habeas corpus*, a requirement that just cause must be shown before a person can be arrested, imprisoned, and tried. Congress could pass no bills of attainder (punishing a person without a jury trial), or pass any *ex post facto* laws (making something a crime after it has taken place). Congress could not tax exports from the various states (goods originating in one state and sent to another for the purpose of trade), or give preference to any port of commerce. In the spirit of the American Revolution, when the colonies had broken with the British monarchy, Congress could not grant any titles of nobility and no citizen could accept titles or gifts from foreign rulers without the consent of Congress.

The Constitution also places limits on the state governments. They cannot enter into treaties or alliances with foreign nations, put their own taxes on exports and imports, or engage in war unless actually invaded. These provisions made the federal government superior to the states in all cases of foreign and military policy. The Constitution also ensured that the United States would become a vast area for free trade. In contrast to the many trade barriers erected among the nations of Europe, American states could not build protectionist walls around themselves by passing laws to tax goods made in other states. These provisions proved a great benefit for the development of American business and industry.

Article 2: The President

Article 2 of the Constitution gives all executive powers to the office of president of the United States. Americans had tried to do without a chief executive under the Articles of Confederation, but the framers believed that the nation needed presidential leadership—so long as the president was carefully checked and balanced by Congress and the judiciary. A president must be at least 35 years old, a natural-born citizen (a native of the United States), and a resident of the United States for at least 14 years. Presidents and vice-presidents serve four-year terms, and may run for reelection as often as they wish. The Twenty-second Amendment (ratified in 1951) limits presidents to no more than two consecutive terms. If a president dies or becomes disabled, then the vice-president assumes the duties of the office.

At first the framers had talked of allowing Congress to pick the president, but they concluded that because the presidency had so many potential powers,

On July 7, 1987, Chairman Daniel Inouye (center, back to camera) administered an oath to Lieutenant Colonel Oliver North (standing) on the first day of North's testimony before the Select Committee on Secret Military Assistance to Iran and the Nicaraguan Opposition. Congress relies heavily on the investigations of its committees to check the president's power.

John Quincy Adams was chosen as the sixth president of the United States by the House of Representatives in 1824 because no candidate had won a majority of the electoral votes. Article 2 of the Constitution grants the House the authority to choose a president in such a situation.

the people should have a role in the president's election. However, instead of direct election of presidents, they decided on an Electoral College. Every state would have the same number of votes in the Electoral College as the number of their senators and representatives. In case no candidate received a majority in the Electoral College, the House of Representatives would decide the election. The House has chosen the president only in 1800 (Thomas Jefferson) and 1824 (John Quincy Adams).

The powers of the president are only briefly described in the Constitution, but they have grown considerably over the past two centuries. The president is commander in chief of the armed forces and is in charge of the civilian agencies of the government as well. Because the president is empowered to receive ambassadors and can decide whether or not to recognize another nation, he is head of state (whereas in England, the monarch is head of state and the prime minister is head of government). The president can negotiate treaties with foreign nations, but treaties must also be ratified by two-thirds of the Senate. The president may also nominate ambassadors, cabinet officers, and judges, but a majority of the Senate must vote to confirm the nominees. The Constitution does not say whether a president can remove a federal officer after Senate confirmation. Later, in 1867, Congress passed a Tenure of Office Act that prohibited presidents from removing an appointed official without the consent of the Senate. When, in 1868, Andrew Johnson fired his secretary of war in violation of this act, the House impeached him, but by a margin of one vote the Senate acquitted him of the charge. The Supreme Court ruled in 1929 that the Tenure of Office Act was unconstitutional.

Every year the president must give information about the state of the Union to Congress. The State of the Union message provides the president the opportunity to propose his legislative program for that year. In the 19th century, presidents sent written messages to Congress. Beginning with Woodrow Wilson in 1913, presidents have appeared in person before a joint session of Congress to deliver their State of the Union addresses. These

In an 1868 cartoon, President Andrew Johnson (far right) tells his opponents that bringing up the issue of his impeachment is equivalent to beating a dead horse. The Senate failed by one vote to convict Johnson of the charges brought against him by the House of Representatives.

personal appearances have served as a symbol of the growing role of the president as "chief legislator," proposing an annual legislative agenda for Congress to adopt, modify, or reject. Presidents can also call Congress back into session in time of emergency. The president is also entrusted to "take care that the laws be faithfully executed," that is, to administer the laws of the nation.

Although Congress passes legislation, the president has a strong hand in the process. Bills become law when the president signs them. If the president does not sign a bill and does not return it within 10 days, it still becomes law. But the president may choose to veto the bill and send it back to Congress along with the reasons for his objections. Both the Senate and House of Representatives must then reconsider the bill and, if approved by a two-thirds roll-call vote in each house, they can override the presidential veto and make the bill law. Because a two-thirds vote is usually difficult to obtain, this makes a veto—or even the threat of a veto—a very powerful presidential weapon.

If the president does not sign a bill and Congress adjourns within 10 days, then the bill dies without any chance of a veto override. This is called a "pocket veto," suggesting that rather than sign it, the president has placed the bill in his pocket. For example, in 1864 Abraham Lincoln pocket vetoed the Wade-Davis bill, which would have established tough policies for readmitting the Southern states to the Union. Lincoln preferred his own more lenient policy and held the Wade-Davis bill until after Congress adjourned to prevent its passage.

Presidents, vice-presidents, federal judges, and any other civil officers of the federal government who commit acts of treason, bribery, or other high crimes and misdemeanors (crimes punishable by imprisonment) may be impeached. The House of Representatives votes to impeach (an action similar to an indictment in court). The Senate, sitting as a court of impeachment, must cast a two-thirds vote to remove that official from office. Impeachment is a difficult procedure that is used only in extreme circumstances. Richard Nixon resigned as president in 1974 rather than face impeachment for his part in the Watergate scandal.

Article 3: The Judiciary

Article 3 provides that judicial power be placed in the control of a Supreme Court and lower federal courts. But the Constitution left it to Congress to establish the federal court system. One of the first acts of Congress was the

President Woodrow Wilson presents his State of the Union message to a joint session of Congress in 1916. Wilson was the first president since John Adams to deliver his legislative agenda in person.

Judiciary Act of 1789, which determined the size of the Supreme Court (consisting of a chief justice and five associate justices), and the number of federal district courts and courts of appeal. (In 1863 the number of Supreme Court justices was increased to nine, as it remains today.) The president appoints all justices of the Supreme Court, and the Senate votes to confirm

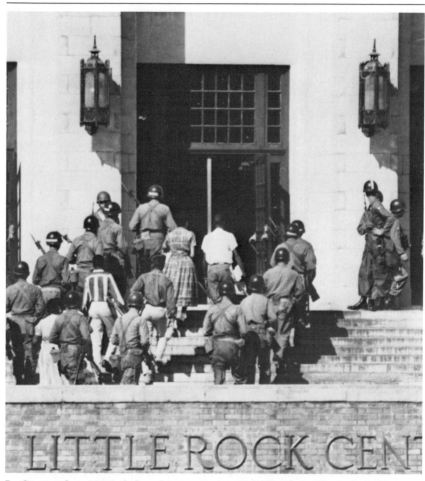

In September 1957, federal troops escorted black students into Central High School in Little Rock, Arkansas. Despite the Supreme Court's 1954 ruling in Brown v. Board of Education of Topeka *that "separate educational facilities are inherently unequal," Governor Faubus refused to permit integration in the state's public schools.*

them. Once appointed, judges are completely independent. They serve until their retirement or death and their salaries may not be reduced. However, they may be impeached for misbehavior.

The Supreme Court and other federal courts have the power to decide cases that arise under the Constitution, federal laws, and treaties. They can decide controversies between two or more states, and between states, citizens, and foreign nations. Except in the case of ambassadors and other foreign representatives, the Supreme Court takes only cases that were first tried in lower courts. Once the Court has ruled, there is no further appeal, except for new legislation. However, the Supreme Court sometimes reexamines the issues and overturns its own precedents. Thus in the 1954 case of *Brown v. Board of Education of Topeka*, the Court refuted earlier decisions that had permitted segregated schools.

The Constitution declares (in Article 6) that the Constitution and laws of the federal government "shall be the supreme Law of the Land." Does this mean that the Supreme Court is the final interpreter of the law? The Constitution makes no mention of "judicial review"—the ability of the Supreme Court to rule an act of Congress unconstitutional. Chief Justice John Marshall asserted this right in the case of *Marbury v. Madison* in 1803, and since then the Supreme Court has argued that such authority is implied by the Constitution. Judicial review is as powerful a tool for the judiciary as the veto is for the president.

Any person accused of a federal crime is guaranteed the right to a trial by jury in Article 3, which also defines treason against the federal government and gives Congress the power to set the punishment for treason.

A major debate over the role of the Supreme Court had focused on the conflicting demands of judicial activism and judicial restraint. Activists believe that a judge should use his or her position to encourage desirable social ends. Those judges who favor restraint, in contrast, hold that a judge's personal philosophy should not be an influence in deciding cases. During the 1920s and 1930s, conservative justices on the Supreme Court pursued an activist policy of striking down social and economic legislation designed to improve conditions for workers and to regulate business. At that time, liberals argued for judicial restraint. In the following decades, however, as more liberal justices were appointed to the Court, liberals came to see the judiciary as a vehicle for ending racial segregation, ensuring voting equality, and protecting individual privacy. By the 1960s, conservatives appealed for judicial restraint. They called for judges to follow the "original intent" of the framers of the Constitution and not to "make law" by rejecting state and federal legislation unless it was clearly

Chief Justice John Marshall explained the Supreme Court's right of judicial review in a landmark case, Marbury v. Madison, *in 1803. Marshall argued that the Supreme Court, as guardian of the Constitution, could declare an act of Congress unconstitutional when it clearly conflicted with the Constitution.*

unconstitutional. Judicial activists responded that the Constitution had created tension between laws and precedents (court rulings that have a bearing on subsequent legal decisions) on one hand and people's current needs and aspirations on the other. They argued that it was left to the Supreme Court to find a balance between these two poles.

Article 4: The States

Article 4 regulates the relations of the states and the federal government. It requires that each state respect the laws and court decisions of other states. This means, for example, that if you drive across the country, your driver's license is legal in all the states. Similarly, a business incorporated in one state can operate in all other states. Article 4 also provides that citizens of the United States are entitled to equal liberties and privileges no matter which state they

CAUTION!!

COLORED PEOPLE

OF BOSTON, ONE & ALL,

You are hereby respectfully CAUTIONED and advised, to avoid conversing with the

Watchmen and Police Officers of Boston,

For since the recent ORDER OF THE MAYOR & ALDERMEN, they are empowered to act as

KIDNAPPERS

AND

Slave Catchers,

And they have already been actually employed in KIDNAPPING, CATCHING, AND KEEPING SLAVES. Therefore, if you value your LIBERTY, and the *Welfare of the Fugitives* among you, *Shun* them in every possible manner, as so many *HOUNDS* on the track of the most unfortunate of your race.

Keep a Sharp Look Out for KIDNAPPERS, and have TOP EYE open.

APRIL 24, 1851.

An 1851 handbill warns blacks in Boston, Massachusetts, about the enforcement of the fugitive slave law, which required that runaway slaves from one state who were captured in another state be returned to their original owners. The fugitive slave law was overturned in 1865 by the Thirteenth Amendment to the Constitution.

57

reside in. These provisions have ensured that the United States has remained one nation and not a collection of hostile states.

If a person commits a crime and flees to another state, the Constitution allows law-enforcement officials to extradite (or legally give back) that person to stand trial in the state where the crime was committed. Originally the Constitution required that slaves ("those held to service or labor") who fled to other states must be returned to their owners. This fugitive slave provision caused much controversy during the years before the Civil War. Southerners demanded that the fugitive slave laws be honored, while Northerners were largely opposed to federal marshals forcing runaway slaves back into slavery. Some abolitionists, such as William Lloyd Garrison, publisher of the newspaper *The Liberator*, who believed slavery was morally wrong and should be immediately abolished, burned copies of the Constitution, denouncing it as a pact with slavery. The fugitive slave provision was revoked by the Thirteenth Amendment, which abolished slavery in 1865.

As pioneers moved west and settled the territories, the Constitution established a mechanism for creating new states. No new state could be formed from within the boundaries of an existing state without the consent of that state's legislature and of Congress. Congress was given authority to make rules and regulations for the territories and to admit them into statehood. Every new state would be equal to the rest of the states.

The Constitution also guaranteed all states "a republican form of government." This meant that people in every state have the right to elect and have a voice in their state government. In addition, the federal government is pledged to help support state governments against domestic (internal) violence.

Articles 6, 7, and 8

Just as the Constitution anticipated that new states would enter the Union, it also expected that new generations would need to amend the Constitution to meet their needs and demands. "The warmest friends and the best supporters the Constitution has do not contend that it is free from imperfection," George Washington wrote to his nephew in 1787, expressing his belief that future Americans would make up their own minds about alterations and amendments. "I do not think we are more inspired, have more wisdom, or possess more virtue than those who will come after us."

Therefore the Constitution set two possible routes for amendment: Two-thirds of the Senate and House may propose an amendment, or two-thirds of the state legislatures can call a convention for proposing amendments. In either case, the amendment must finally be ratified by three-quarters of the state legislatures before it is added to the Constitution. This is a complicated process

When President Thomas Jefferson purchased the Louisiana Territory in 1803, he put serious stress on the Constitution, which said nothing about acquiring foreign territory. Jefferson, using the so-called elastic clause of the Constitution, which gave Congress power to make all laws necessary and proper to carry out government business, persuaded Congress to approve the acquisition of the land.

requiring a national consensus. It helps to explain why Americans have been reluctant to make many changes in the Constitution. Of the hundreds of amendments suggested over the years, only 26 have been approved.

Article 6 promised that the new government would assume all the debts of the Continental Congress during the American Revolution and of the Congress under the Articles of Confederation. This provision helped convince the nation's creditors of the need to ratify the new Constitution. Article 6 also calls on all federal and state officeholders to take an oath to support the Constitution and prohibits any religious requirements for holding office. Section 2, the "Supremacy Clause," declares the Constitution to be "the supreme Law of the Land." This clause was designed to keep the states from passing laws that conflict with the Constitution.

Finally, the framers of the Constitution were aware that amending the Articles of Confederation required a unanimous vote of the states, which was extremely difficult to achieve. Therefore, Article 7 stated that only 9 of the 13 states would be needed to ratify the Constitution.

Enumerated and Implied Powers

The Constitution is a relatively short document, far shorter than many state constitutions. Written in the 18th century, it has shown its flexibility by growing along with the nation and meeting new social and economic challenges of expansion, war, depression, and industrial and technological change. Yet for all its flexibility, the Constitution has also acted as a restraint on arbitrary power and has preserved and protected the liberties of U.S. citizens.

In addition to separation of powers, the framers attempted to restrict the federal government to those duties specifically enumerated (listed) in the Constitution. They expected that the states would exercise all other powers. However, the framers also wrote the "elastic clause" into the Constitution, giving Congress power to make all laws necessary and proper to carry out government business. This vague provision has enabled the government to stretch its powers far beyond those enumerated in the Constitution. Those who believe that a loose construction is necessary to adapt the Constitution to modern problems argue that these are "implied powers."

Under implied powers, President Thomas Jefferson purchased the Louisiana Territory, although the Constitution says nothing about acquiring new land. During the 1930s, Congress enacted unprecedented spending programs to give relief and employment to the victims of the depression. And in 1950

President Harry Truman sent American troops into combat in Korea without a declaration of war (thus not requiring the consent of Congress).

Some have argued that these extensions of power were vital to the national interest. Others worry that the federal government has grown too large and powerful at the expense of states' rights and call for a stricter construction of the Constitution. Opponents of government growth have urged the courts to pay more attention to the "original intent" of the framers of the Constitution. The debate between strict and loose constructionists has continued for 200 years and has helped to focus each generation's attention on the remarkable system of separation of powers, checks and balances, and enumerated and implied powers embodied in the Constitution of the United States.

The Bill of Rights, the first 10 amendments to the Constitution, lists the rights a person possesses that cannot be violated by the government. The Bill of Rights was added to the Constitution as a condition for its ratification by the states on the insistence of delegates who had misgivings about a strong central government.

FIVE

The Bill of Rights

James Madison had at first been skeptical of the need for a bill of rights in the Constitution. He believed that the people's rights were already protected by the various state constitutions. But when the Anti-Federalists campaigned against ratification of the Constitution on the grounds that a strong central government might restrict individual rights, Madison promised to work to amend the Constitution as soon as possible. When Madison was elected to the first House of Representatives, he proved true to his word. In June 1789, Madison introduced in Congress the amendments that became the Bill of Rights.

Why bother to change a Constitution that had just been ratified? Some congressmen argued that if they simply went about their business and passed good laws, then public fears would subside. But Madison replied that there were still many citizens who expressed dissatisfaction with the Constitution. Indeed, two states—Rhode Island and North Carolina—had not yet ratified it. Critics of the Constitution were patriotic people who wanted to protect their liberties, said Madison: "They may think we are not sincere in our desire to incorporate such amendments in the Constitution as will secure those rights which they consider as not sufficiently guarded."

Despite a busy legislative workload, which involved turning the provisions of the Constitution into a functioning government, the House eventually adopted a series of amendments to the Constitution. The Senate accepted all of these but one. To Madison's dismay, the Senate rejected an amendment that would have made the liberties embodied in the Bill of Rights binding on the states. Thus for nearly a century, the Bill of Rights protected people's liberties only from encroachment by the federal government and not by the states. The Fourteenth Amendment, ratified in 1868, applied the Bill of Rights to the states. It declared that no state should "make or enforce any law which shall abridge the privileges or immunities of citizens of the United States" and promised every citizen "equal protection of the laws." However, it has required numerous Supreme Court decisions in the 20th century to uphold the specific freedoms of the Bill of Rights against the laws of the states.

Congress sent 12 amendments out to the states, which ratified only 10. The two rejected amendments dealt not with individual liberties but with the apportionment of the House of Representatives (allocation of legislative seats according to population) and with the salaries of members of Congress. Had the apportionment amendment been ratified, over the years as the population grew the size of the House would have swelled to unmanageable proportions. Had the salary amendment been approved, it would have prohibited any congressional pay raise from taking place during the Congress that approved it. This might have eased the politically unpopular chore of voting to raise one's own salary.

The 10 amendments that became part of the Constitution in 1791 constituted the largest change in the original document. Later amendments were added one by one, with many years elapsing between them.

The First Amendment

The First Amendment includes five major liberties: freedom of religion, speech, the press, to assemble peacefully, and to petition the government. It declares that "Congress shall make no law respecting an establishment of religion, or prohibiting the free exercise thereof." In many nations, a single religion became the official state religion. Those citizens who were not members of that religion were denied civil rights and otherwise persecuted for their beliefs. England had undergone centuries of religious struggle between Protestants and Catholics and many of the first immigrants to the British colonies in America were Protestant dissenters from the established Church of England. Jews were persecuted throughout Europe, and Christians and Moslems had long clashed in the Middle East. The First Amendment sought to avoid such sectarian warfare in the United States by prohibiting any one

Mr. and Mrs. Edward Schempp and their family are shown on the steps of the U.S. Supreme Court in Washington, D.C. The Schempps challenged the Pennsylvania law requiring that at least 10 verses of the Bible be read without comment at the beginning of each school day. In 1963, the Court declared the law an unconstitutional violation of the First Amendment and argued that although the study of religion could be included in a school's curriculum, a public school could not be used for religious purposes.

religion from becoming the official state religion and by protecting every individual's right to worship as he or she desires. This amendment has also kept the government from taxing church property or from giving federal aid to religious schools.

The First Amendment also prohibits the government from abridging, or restricting, the freedoms of speech and of the press. The rights to speak out for one's beliefs and to publish pamphlets and newspapers had been critical elements in rousing public sentiment behind the American Revolution. Americans also remembered with pride the case of John Peter Zenger, the colonial

65

John Peter Zenger (in the witness stand at the right), publisher of The New-York Weekly Journal, *was arrested for libel, or publishing a false statement damaging to a person's reputation, when he criticized the royal governor of New York in 1735. Zenger's lawyer offered the defense that Zenger had told the truth in his articles and that freedom of speech for the English people was at stake. A jury acquitted Zenger of the charges.*

printer who in 1735 was acquitted by a jury for criticizing the royal governor of New York. Zenger had argued that his charges against the governor were true and that free speech was the right of all British citizens. The Constitution ensured that these freedoms would also be the rights of all Americans.

Although the language of the First Amendment seems absolute when it says that "Congress shall make no law respecting an establishment of religion, or prohibiting the free exercise thereof; or abridging the freedom of speech, or of the press; or the right of the people peaceably to assemble, and to petition the Government for a redress of grievances," both Congress and the courts have at times felt the need to define and limit the freedoms of speech and of the press. The Supreme Court has ruled that freedom of speech is not a license to yell "Fire!" in a crowded theater when there is no fire. For this reason, in 1919, in the *Schenck v. United States* case, the Supreme Court ruled against Schenck, who was general secretary of the Socialist party and who, in a speech during World War I, told men to avoid the draft for military service because he believed the war was a capitalist conspiracy. Justice Oliver Wendell Holmes, Jr., wrote the opinion for the court, which became known as the "clear and present danger" test, stating that some things that could be uttered publicly in peacetime could not be expressed in wartime when those things would produce a "clear and present danger" to the country. The Schenck decision has been applied by the courts as the basis for determining restrictions on the constitutionally guaranteed freedom of expression.

Frequently, newspapers have angered government officials either by criticizing their policies or by publishing information that the officials felt harmed the national security. In 1798, Congress passed the Alien and Sedition Acts, which were designed by the Federalist party to curb criticism of the government by Republican newspapers and their editors, many of whom were foreign-born. The acts authorized the president to deport undesirable aliens and made it a crime to criticize the government or its officials. Some newspaper editors went to jail for writing articles critical of President John Adams and the Federalist majority in Congress. These acts proved highly unpopular and contributed to the Federalists' defeat at the polls when Thomas Jefferson won the presidency in 1800. The new Republican majority allowed the Alien and Sedition laws to expire. In 1971, the Supreme Court ruled against the Nixon administration's attempts to stop the *New York Times* from publishing still-secret documents known as the "Pentagon Papers." The Court ruled that the First Amendment protected the newspapers from such "prior restraint" on their decisions about what news to print.

The rights to assemble peaceably and to petition the government assure citizens the chance to protest against government policies they consider wrong or unjust. Under these rights, abolitionists sent great numbers of petitions signed by many citizens throughout the North protesting against slavery. Other citizens have petitioned to settle small private claims against the government, or to register their support or disapproval of any number of current issues. The National Archives preserves hundreds of thousands of such petitions that the government has received over the past two centuries. Citizens may also assemble peacefully to demonstrate their feelings on an issue. Exercising this right, Dr. Martin Luther King, Jr., led a "March on Washington" for civil rights in 1963, and antiwar demonstrators protested against the Vietnam War. In some cases, communities have found the particular issues supported by demonstrators to be offensive and have tried to stop them, but the courts have generally upheld the right to assemble peacefully, no matter what the cause.

The Second, Third, and Fourth Amendments

The next three amendments reflect issues that had aroused public concern at the time of the American Revolution. The Second Amendment declares that because "a well-regulated militia" is necessary for the security of a free state, "the right of the people to keep and bear arms shall not be infringed." Opponents of gun control legislation cite the Second Amendment in opposition to efforts to limit the number of guns in society. They believe that individuals have a constitutional right to arm themselves for self-protection. Supporters of gun control interpret the same amendment as protecting not the rights of individual citizens to own guns but those of the militia (state military forces made up of civilians). The courts have ruled that this amendment does not prevent the government from establishing regulations for the ownership of guns.

Under the Third Amendment, the government cannot force citizens to lodge troops in their homes without their consent. This was the result of grievances against the British, who quartered troops in people's homes in the years prior to the Revolution. Similarly, Americans remembered how the British had searched homes and property looking for smuggled goods. The Fourth Amendment prohibits the government from conducting any "unreasonable searches and seizures" without proper warrants (written orders) from the courts.

The Fifth Amendment

One of the most controversial amendments in the Bill of Rights is the Fifth Amendment, which protects the rights of people accused of committing crimes. People who are unhappy with the courts for pampering, or "coddling," criminals, often wish that the government would take tougher actions against suspected criminals, but the Constitution explicitly restricts the ways in which government can act in criminal cases. These restrictions are designed to ensure that everyone gets a fair trial and the innocent are not falsely convicted.

Dr. Martin Luther King, Jr. (foreground, center), exercising the right to assemble peacefully, leads a 1963 march in Washington, D.C. More than 250,000 people from across the nation participated in the demonstration, which was planned by civil rights supporters to promote the passage of civil rights legislation introduced in Congress.

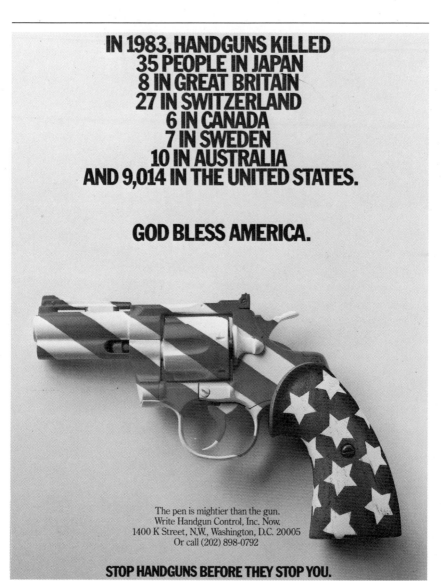

IN 1983, HANDGUNS KILLED
35 PEOPLE IN JAPAN
8 IN GREAT BRITAIN
27 IN SWITZERLAND
6 IN CANADA
7 IN SWEDEN
10 IN AUSTRALIA
AND 9,014 IN THE UNITED STATES.

GOD BLESS AMERICA.

The pen is mightier than the gun.
Write Handgun Control, Inc. Now.
1400 K Street, N.W., Washington, D.C. 20005
Or call (202) 898-0792

STOP HANDGUNS BEFORE THEY STOP YOU.

A 1983 poster urges support for the control of handguns, focusing on the number of people killed by such weapons in the United States in one year—9,014. The Second Amendment to the Constitution gives Americans the right to bear arms; however, supporters of gun control interpret the amendment as protecting the right of the militia, not that of individual citizens, to own guns.

In addition to the Fourth Amendment's requirement for a warrant describing the reason and place of a search, the Fifth Amendment provides that a person charged with a major crime must be first indicted, or charged with a crime by a grand jury (a jury of 12 to 23 members that examines accusations against a person charged with a crime and decides whether or not to make formal charges against the accused), before being brought to trial. A person cannot be tried a second time for a crime he or she was found innocent of committing. No one may be forced to answer questions that might incriminate him-or herself. The government cannot seize a person's property without just compensation. And no person "shall be deprived of life, liberty, or property, without due process of law"—that is, the right to a trial.

The spirit of the Fifth Amendment emphasizes that any person accused of a crime is innocent until proven guilty in a court of law. At times this precaution makes it seem as if the courts care more about the perpetrators of a crime than its victims. But citizens are guaranteed the right to due process of the law, no matter how guilty they may appear, or how terrible the crime they have been accused of committing.

Similarly, the right not to give testimony against oneself became the subject of public outcry during the anti-Communist investigations held by congressional committees in the 1940s and 1950s. When witnesses refused to admit whether they had ever been members of the Communist party, or to "name names" of other possible Communists, some members of Congress and newspaper commentators concluded that a refusal to testify was an admission of guilt. However, the Fifth Amendment has remained a strong protector of the rights of anyone justly or unjustly accused.

The Sixth, Seventh, and Eighth Amendments

The rights of the accused are further protected by the Sixth Amendment, which states that everyone is entitled to a speedy and public trial. Accused people may not be kept languishing under prolonged indictments, nor may they be tried in secret. They have a right to a fair trial by an impartial jury and they must be told about the charges against them. They must have the right to face all witnesses who testify against them. They must be able to subpoena (to force by court order) people who can testify in their favor. And they have a right to have a lawyer to defend them.

71

In 1963, the Supreme Court ruled in *Gideon v. Wainwright* that the Sixth Amendment's right to counsel was not limited by a person's ability to pay a lawyer's fee. The Court ruled that Clarence Gideon was denied a fair trial because he could not afford a lawyer and that thereafter the state must provide public defenders for the poor.

The Seventh Amendment requires trial by jury in civil cases where one individual sues another for any amount of money more than $20. (Small claims, such as disputes over grocery bills or wages, are settled in small claims courts by a judge instead of a jury in order to facilitate minor cases and to save money.) The Eighth Amendment prohibits the courts from setting excessive bail to keep accused people in prison pending their trials, or from imposing excessive fines. It also forbids "cruel and unusual punishment." This prohibition was intended to prevent the torture of prisoners, but the Supreme Court has ruled that the death penalty is not "cruel and unusual punishment."

The Ninth and Tenth Amendments

The Ninth and Tenth amendments deal with rights of the people and of the states not mentioned in the Constitution or the Bill of Rights. People's rights are not limited to those that appear in the Constitution. The Tenth Amendment reserves for the states all powers not specifically granted to the federal government. Supporters of "states' rights" have frequently cited the Tenth Amendment when they argue that the federal government has grown too powerful. They believe that the states have jurisdiction over any issue not specifically mentioned in the Constitution, such as education. But those who believe in a more active federal government believe that the "elastic clause" (Article 1, Section 8, Clause 18) permits the federal government to make all laws "necessary and proper" to "promote the general welfare."

Although the right of the states as expressed in the Tenth Amendment has been eroded over the years by an ever-expanding central government, the states are still an important part of American federalism. Local and state governments are closer to the people who elect them and have major responsibilities, particularly in such areas as education, health, and economic development. During the Progressive era (c.1890–1916), reformers saw the states as "social laboratories" that could pioneer in enacting reform measures in advance of the federal government. Finally, through their senators and representatives in Washington, the states also have a voice in the federal system.

In 1950, Senator Joseph McCarthy (back row, far right) listens to a witness testify before a Senate committee investigating the loyalty of State Department officals who were alleged Communists. Many witnesses invoked the Fifth Amendment, which protects a person's right not to give testimony against him- or herself.

Safeguards of the Bill of Rights

During the 20th century the safeguards of individual liberties in the Bill of Rights have continually been strengthened by Supreme Court decisions. Rulings have extended the restraints of the Bill of Rights to the states as well as to the federal government. For example, in *Gitlow v. New York* in 1925, the Supreme Court declared that freedom of speech and of the press, protected by the First Amendment, were "among the fundamental personal rights and 'liberties' protected by the due process clause of the Fourteenth Amendment from impact by the states."

Yet there have also been setbacks. Following the attack on Pearl Harbor in 1941, anti-Japanese sentiments ran so high on the West Coast that the government forcibly removed more than 120,000 Japanese-Americans from their homes and businesses and moved them to isolated relocation camps. The president, Congress, and the Supreme Court agreed to this violation of civil rights, citing the nation's need for security in time of war. In later years, the government came to regret its action, but by then irreparable damage had been done to thousands of innocent people. (The Japanese-Americans who were held in the camps during the war filed a lawsuit in 1984, seeking compensation

Under a 1942 U.S. Army war emergency order, Japanese-Americans were evacuated from their California homes and placed in internment camps. Congress, President Roosevelt, and the Supreme Court agreed to the violation of these citizens' civil rights, in part reacting to the public's fear of sabotage during wartime.

74

from the government for property losses.) Similarly, in the 1950s a wave of anti-Communism endangered the rights of free speech, free press, and freedom to petition along with other civil liberties. This movement took the name of "McCarthyism," after Senator Joseph McCarthy of Wisconsin who alleged that he had a list of names of 205 Communists in the State Department. Witnesses were harassed and careers were destroyed in the senator's and his colleagues' drive to root out Communist subversion.

Thus, although the Bill of Rights has become more strongly entrenched than ever, Americans can never take their rights for granted. Popular passions for seemingly righteous causes may well erode the most fundamental rights. Protection of these rights is a matter not just for governments but for the vigilance of all citizens.

In 1967, Thurgood Marshall was the first black appointed an associ-ate justice of the Supreme Court. In his comments about the 1987 bi-centennial celebration of the Constitution, Justice Marshall referred to the Constitution as a "living document" because it continues to grow and change in order to meet the challenges of modern society.

SIX

The Living Constitution

Justice Thurgood Marshall expressed his strong personal reservations about how to celebrate the bicentennial of the Constitution in 1987. As the first black member of the Supreme Court, Marshall did not accept the notion that the Philadelphia convention had forever "fixed" the Constitution, nor did he particularly admire the framers' wisdom and sense of justice. He believed that their compromise with slavery had made a government that was "defective from the start" and that required several amendments, a civil war, and the civil rights movement to develop a federal system that respected the individual freedoms and human rights of all its citizens. But he also recognized that the United States had made great progress toward equal justice under law in the 200 years since the Constitution was drafted. Justice Marshall concluded that he would "celebrate the bicentennial of the Constitution as a living document, including the Bill of Rights and other amendments protecting individual freedoms and human rights."

The Constitution is a "living" document because of its ability to grow and change to meet new conditions facing new generations. Since the adoption of the Bill of Rights in 1791, another 16 amendments have been added to the Constitution—4 of which especially broadened the rights of black Americans and women. But amendments are not the only way in which the Constitution changes. Laws passed by Congress, actions taken by presidents, and decisions made by the Supreme Court have all altered our interpretations and applications of the Constitution. Throughout American history there has been considerable debate within the nation about what the Constitution means and how it should be carried out. This tension, between those who want a more active government and those who insist on government restraints, has helped to balance the federal government in meeting the needs of the people and preserving their basic liberties.

Presidents and Congress

After the Constitution was adopted, Americans elected George Washington as their first president and gave to him the responsibility of establishing the executive branch and setting the precedents that other presidents would follow. Washington appointed a cabinet, or group of heads of the executive departments (the Secretary of State, Secretary of the Treasury, Secretary of War, Attorney General, and Postmaster General), although no such cabinet was specifically mentioned in the Constitution. Starting with Washington's five cabinet secretaries, along with a few clerks, the executive departments have now expanded into a vast bureaucracy, touching every area of American life. The Constitution does not elaborate on a president's relations with Congress, but Washington proposed legislation for Congress to enact. And at the end of his second term, Washington decided to retire, although he could easily have won reelection. This set a two-term tradition (broken only when Franklin Roosevelt was elected four times) that is now written into the Constitution as law.

During the first half of the 19th century the Constitution became a battleground between the North and South over the issue of slavery. As politicians such as Senator Henry Clay of Kentucky tried to find compromises to cool passions on both sides, Senator John C. Calhoun of South Carolina rebutted that the Constitution was a rock on which the nation could better stand "than on the shifting sands of compromise. Let us be done with compromises. Let us go back and stand on the Constitution."

The Constitution made no provisions for states to leave the Union after they had joined, but the debate over slavery had become so intense that after the election of 1860, 11 states seceded from the Union. In January 1861, U.S. army colonel Robert E. Lee wrote sadly to his son that "Secession is nothing

President George Washington (left) and the heads of his cabinet departments: from left, Henry Knox, Secretary of War; Alexander Hamilton, Secretary of the Treasury; Edmund Randolph, Attorney General; and Thomas Jefferson, Secretary of State. Although a presidential cabinet is not expressly mentioned in the Constitution, Washington set up executive departments and appointed their heads with the consent of the Senate.

but revolution. The framers of our Constitution never exhausted so much labor, wisdom and forbearance in its formation, and surrounded it with so many guards and securities, if it was intended to be broken by any member of the Confederacy at will." Lee later joined the Confederate army only to defend his native state of Virginia.

During the Civil War, President Abraham Lincoln assumed sweeping powers and severely curtailed civil liberties. Civilian opponents of the war were arrested and held without trial or were tried by military courts. Critical newspapers were closed down. Lincoln believed that in such a time of emergency it was necessary to take unconstitutional steps in order to save the Constitution by preserving the nation and government it created. The Congress supported Lincoln's extreme measures, but became impatient with

Senator John C. Calhoun of South Carolina was an uncompromising spokesman for slavery in debates concerning the expansion of slavery into federal territories. To support his belief in the southerner's right to own slaves, he referred to Article 1, section 9, of the Constitution, which had allowed the South to maintain slavery until 1865.

his lenient policies toward the South. After Lincoln's assassination in 1865, Congress clashed sharply with President Andrew Johnson over Reconstruction policies. In 1868, the Senate failed by one vote to remove Johnson from office.

In the later years of the 19th century many in Congress interpreted the role of the presidency narrowly. They believed that the president's role was limited to carrying out the laws passed by Congress. Congress played an aggressive role in leadership and few presidents offered much resistance. The chain of relatively weak presidents was broken at the beginning of the 20th century when a young and vigorous Theodore Roosevelt entered the White House. The first of the modern activist presidents, Roosevelt believed that a president had a duty "to do anything that the nation demanded unless such action was forbidden by the Constitution or by law." His successor, William Howard Taft, took the opposite position. Taft argued that a president could only do what could be "fairly and justly implied and included" in the Constitution.

But most 20th-century presidents have followed Roosevelt's lead, and the power of the presidency grew steadily, especially as the United States became more militarily and diplomatically significant in world affairs. By the 1970s, Congress became troubled over the development of an "imperial presidency." They objected when President Nixon impounded (refused to spend) funds that Congress had appropriated and sent troops into combat without consulting them. In 1973 Congress passed the War Powers Act to limit the president's authority to commit troops overseas without congressional approval and, in 1974, the Budget Act to prohibit impoundment of funds.

Another gray area between the presidency and Congress was the development of such independent regulatory agencies as the Federal Trade Commission (established in 1914 to restrict unethical business practices in interstate and foreign commerce and to promote fair competition) and the Securities and Exchange Commission (created in 1934 to regulate the buying of securities— stocks and bonds), which the Constitution did not envision. In an effort to

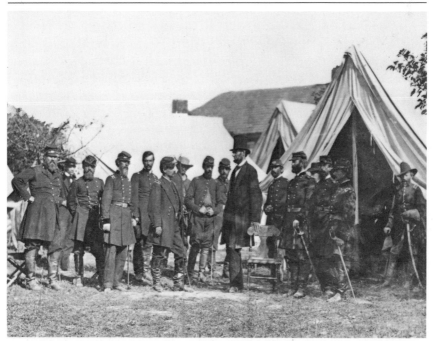

President Abraham Lincoln (center) visits General George B. McClellan, commander of the Army of the Potomac, during the Civil War. In order to preserve the Union, Lincoln believed it was necessary to curtail several civil liberties, such as the writ of habeas corpus and freedom of the press.

regulate complex economic issues, Congress created independent agencies that combined executive, legislative, and judicial functions for more efficiency and effectiveness. Some saw these agencies as a violation of the separation of powers. However, their defenders have argued that they are within the scope of the Constitution because the president appoints all commissioners, Congress funds and oversees their activities, and the courts judge the legality of their actions.

Judicial Review

The Constitution also changes through federal court interpretation. Beginning with *Marbury v. Madison* in 1803, the Supreme Court has asserted its authority to declare acts of Congress unconstitutional, a principle known as judicial review. The Federalists had commissioned William Marbury to be a justice of the peace in Washington, D.C. The new Republican secretary of state, James Madison, decided not to deliver the commission to Marbury, who then petitioned the Supreme Court for a court order demanding his commission. Chief Justice John Marshall wrote in his opinion that Madison did not have the right to refuse the commission of a properly appointed official, but he concluded that the Supreme Court had no authority to issue a court order because the Constitution had not included the issue of court orders to executive officers in defining the original jurisdiction of the Supreme Court. Therefore, the Court declared the portion of the Judiciary Act of 1789 that gave it such authority to be unconstitutional.

Marbury v. Madison was a landmark case in determining the right of the Supreme Court to rule on constitutionality. For the first time, an act of Congress was declared unconstitutional. The Supreme Court has relied heavily on Marshall's opinion in articulating the doctrine of judicial review: that it is the duty of the Supreme Court to determine what the law is and to repeal statutes that are "contrary to the Constitution."

In 1819, Chief Justice Marshall wrote the opinion for another significant case, *McCulloch v. Maryland*, which dealt with a state's attempt to tax the federally chartered Bank of the United States. Marshall explained that the people, not the states, had created the Constitution. Under this reasoning the federal government was superior to the states and thus not subject to taxation by them. Moreover, while the Constitution had made no mention of any Bank of the United States, Marshall ruled that the Constitution gave the government power to control the currency and did not prevent it from chartering a bank for

The slave Dred Scott sued for his freedom when he was returned to a slave state after having lived in a free state. In 1857, the Supreme Court ruled in Dred Scott v. Sandford *that Scott had not become a free person when he was taken by his master to a free state. Furthermore, the Court ruled that because blacks were not citizens of the United States they could not sue in a federal court.*

assistance. In his ruling, John Marshall leaned heavily upon the "elastic clause" and supported a loose construction of the Constitution rather than relying upon its enumerated powers.

As the issue of slavery threatened to divide the nation, the Supreme Court attempted to resolve the problem with its decision in *Dred Scott v. Sandford* in 1857. The Court ruled that the slave Dred Scott had not become a free person when he entered free territory, because black Americans were not citizens. The Court further ruled that Congress could not prohibit slavery in the territories, because slaveholders could not be denied their right to own property. Instead of settling the issue, however, the *Dred Scott* decision only angered the North and pushed the nation closer to civil war. The Thirteenth Amendment, abolishing slavery, eventually nullified the *Dred Scott* decision.

After the Civil War, the Fourteenth Amendment was ratified. This amendment permitted the Supreme Court to extend the protection of the Bill of Rights to supersede the authority of the states. Congress enacted civil rights laws to protect the newly freed people in the South. But in 1883 the Supreme Court ruled these laws unconstitutional. Then in 1896 the Court ruled against

The For Colored Only sign posted next to a drinking fountain in the South illustrates the doctrine of "separate but equal" accommodations that were legally allowed under the Constitution until 1964.

Homer Plessy, who was refused a first-class seat in a railroad car because he was black. In the case of *Plessy v. Ferguson*, the Court ruled that "separate but equal" accommodations were legal. This ruling made racial segregation legal for the next 70 years.

By contrast, in the late 19th century the Supreme Court extended sympathetic treatment to business corporations. In 1886 the court struck down state railroad laws on the grounds that the states could not regulate an interstate business. It was in reaction to this decision that Congress established the first independent regulatory commission, the Interstate Commerce Commission, to regulate railroads.

The Supreme Court's sympathy for business and suspicion of government regulation led to its major clash with the administration of President Franklin D. Roosevelt. The Court ruled that Congress had delegated too much of its power to New Deal agencies, such as the National Recovery Agency, created to bring an end to the depression. President Roosevelt, who was the first president in more than a century who had served a full term without having the opportunity to appoint a single justice to the Supreme Court, sought to change the Court by adding as many as 6 new justices to assist those justices over the age of 70. Roosevelt's opponents called this a plan to "pack" the Supreme Court in an attempt to weaken the judiciary. Arguing against judicial activism, Roosevelt pointed out that "the Constitution is what the justices say it is rather than what its framers or you might hope it is." Despite the large Democratic majority in Congress, there was great opposition to the president's plan, which both conservatives and progressives saw as an assault on the Constitution. Roosevelt suffered a stunning defeat on his Court plan, although in later years

A 1937 cartoon lampoons President Franklin Roosevelt's plan to name six additional justices to the Supreme Court in an attempt to sway the direction of the Court's decisions. However, there was great hostility toward the plan in Congress, where many members considered it an attack on the Constitution itself.

he was able to name eight of the nine justices, and thereby change the direction of the Court.

When President Dwight D. Eisenhower nominated Earl Warren to be Chief Justice in 1953, he believed that Warren would follow a moderate course on the Court. But Warren helped move the Court in a liberal activist direction. In 1954 the Court unanimously reversed itself on segregation. In *Brown v. Board of Education of Topeka* it ruled "separate but equal" schools unconstitutional and ordered schools to desegregate "with all deliberate speed." In the 1960s, the Warren Court made a series of bold decisions that protected the rights of criminal defendants. It declared that police could not use evidence obtained without a search warrant, nor could they use confessions given if the defendant had not been allowed to see a lawyer.

In the case of *Baker v. Carr* in 1962, the Court ruled in favor of "one man, one vote." Previously, smaller populated rural districts had more representation in state legislatures than did heavily populated urban districts. The Court said that states must apportion their legislatures so that districts were divided evenly. Also in 1962, the Supreme Court ruled in *Engel v. Vitale* that public schools violated the First Amendment when they required students to recite a daily prayer.

Chief Justice Earl Warren (seated, center) and associate justices of the Supreme Court. Warren moved the Court in a liberal direction instead of the moderate one hoped for by President Eisenhower. In 1954, the Warren Court ruled unanimously that "separate but equal" schools for blacks and whites were unconstitutional.

Many of these Supreme Court decisions were unpopular and became political issues. Richard Nixon campaigned against the "permissive" attitudes of the Warren Court toward criminal defendants. He promised to appoint "strict constructionists" to the Supreme Court. (Strict constructionists are those judges who favor a strict interpretation of the Constitution, granting as much power as possible to the states. In contrast, loose constructionists have a more liberal interpretation, believing that the national government is granted broad, or implied, powers.) His appointees did help swing the majority on the Supreme Court in favor of the death penalty and in support of greater police powers instead of the civil liberties of the accused. But they did not reverse the Warren Court indiscriminately. Depending heavily on precedents, the Supreme Court has always been reluctant to abandon the collected decisions of previous courts.

Amendments to the Constitution

A Supreme Court decision is not necessarily the final word on any issue. If Congress takes exception to a Court ruling, it can enact new statutes, or even offer amendments to the Constitution. The Eleventh Amendment, adopted in 1798, came in reaction to the Supreme Court's decision in *Chisholm v. Georgia* that federal courts could hear suits brought by citizens against their states. The new amendment reversed this decision and stated that such cases should be tried only in state courts.

The Twelfth Amendment (1804) sought to avoid a repetition of the fight over the 1800 presidential election. Both Thomas Jefferson, the presidential candidate, and his running mate for the vice-presidency, Aaron Burr, received the same number of electoral votes. The Constitution had established that each elector vote for two candidates for the office of president; the candidate who won the majority of the votes won the presidency. However, the Constitution had made no provision for a situation that resulted in a tie. Article 2 of the Constitution stipulated that when there was no candidate with a clear majority of the ballots the House was to choose the president from a list containing the names of the five candidates who had received the most votes. The election was thrown into the House of Representatives, which cast some 40 ballots before it elected Jefferson president. The new amendment required the electoral college to cast separate votes for president and vice-president, specifying by name the person voted for as president and the person voted for as vice-president.

On January 31, 1865, members of the House of Representatives jubi-lantly celebrate the passage of the Thirteenth Amendment, which abolished slavery in the United States.

After the Civil War, the Thirteenth (1865), Fourteenth (1868), and Fifteenth (1870) amendments were added to the Constitution, abolishing slavery, extending due process of the law to the states, and giving black men the right to vote. Both the Thirteenth and Fourteenth amendments had "enforcement" clauses, giving Congress the power to enforce the amendments' provisions by specific legislation. Many civil rights bills have drawn their constitutionality from these enforcement clauses. The scope of the Fourteenth Amendment has caused much disagreement among historians, lawyers, and judges. Those who favor a narrower interpretation of the Constitution have argued that the authors of the Fourteenth Amendment had intended only to incorporate into the Constitution the Civil Rights Act of 1866 and to protect the rights of the newly freed slaves. Those favoring a broader interpretation believe the authors of the amendment intended it to apply the entire Bill of Rights to the states.

During the Progressive era at the beginning of the 20th century, several reforms were written into the Constitution. The Sixteenth Amendment (1913) made a federal income tax legal. Although income taxes had been levied during the Civil War, the Supreme Court had ruled in 1895 that they were unconstitutional on the ground that an income tax was a direct tax and Congress should have apportioned it among the states according to population as stated in the Constitution (Article 1, section 9). As a result of the Sixteenth Amendment the government could collect more revenue and provide more services. The Seventeenth Amendment (1913) gave voters the right to elect their senators directly, rather than through their state legislatures, a system that had become scandal-ridden. The Eighteenth Amendment (1918) prohibited the sale of alcoholic beverages. And the Nineteenth Amendment (1920) capped the long women's suffrage movement by giving women the right to vote.

Prohibition, as the Eighteenth Amendment was called, had long been advocated by women's rights groups, temperance leaders (people who promoted moderation in or abstinence from the use of alcohol), and reformers who believed that drunkenness destroyed people's lives. But during the 1920s Prohibition was openly flouted—public opinion had reversed itself. The Twenty-first Amendment (1933) repealed Prohibition. The Eighteenth Amendment is not the only clause of the Constitution to be repealed. Several sections in the original Constitution were voided by later amendments, for example, the Eighteenth Amendment, and the Fourteenth Amendment's references to voters as "male inhabitants . . . being twenty-one years of age" were repealed by amendments giving the right to vote to women and to 18 year olds.

The Twentieth Amendment (1933) ended "lame duck" sessions of the Congress. Written in an era when communication and transportation were slow, the original Constitution had set the first Monday in December as the opening day of each session of Congress. This meant that more than a year elapsed between an election and the end of the terms of those defeated or retired in that election, known as "lame duck" senators and representatives. These "lame ducks," who were now no longer responsible to the voting public, often blocked reform legislation. Presidential terms did not begin until March 4, resulting in a four-month wait after the election before the new president

In Philadelphia, an officer destroys barrels of beer after the sale of alcoholic beverages was banned by the Eighteenth Amendment in 1918. Prohibition was repealed in 1933 by the Twenty-first Amendment.

Suffragettes campaign in New Jersey. Until the passage of the Nineteenth Amendment in 1920, women were unable to vote in elections.

could take office. The Twentieth Amendment moved the opening day of Congress to January 3 and the inauguration of the president from March 4 to January 20.

When Franklin D. Roosevelt broke George Washington's two-term tradition and won third and fourth terms as president, Congress reacted by proposing the Twenty-second Amendment (1951), which limits presidents to no more than two elected terms. The Constitution had also provided that Congress would administer the seat of the federal government, located in the District of Columbia, but citizens of the District were unable to vote in federal elections. The Twenty-third Amendment (1961) gave District residents the right to vote for president. Because the District is not a state, its residents cannot elect senators and have only a non-voting delegate in the House of Representatives.

As the civil rights movement gained strength in the 1960s and pressed for equal rights for minorities, the Twenty-fourth Amendment (1964) was proposed to abolish the poll tax, a fee that many southern states charged to people

91

who wished to vote, as a way of discouraging blacks and the poor—including whites—from voting. The assassination of President Kennedy in 1963 left the vice-presidency vacant for more than a year. Concerned about a more orderly presidential succession, Congress drafted the Twenty-fifth Amendment (1967), which permits presidents to nominate someone to fill a vacancy in the vice-presidency, subject to confirmation by the Senate. It also creates a mechanism for the vice-president to assume the presidency in case the president becomes disabled. Within a decade after the Twenty-fifth Amendment was ratified it was employed twice. Both Gerald Ford and Nelson Rockefeller were appointed and confirmed as vice-president under this amendment.

The most recent amendment to the Constitution, the Twenty-sixth (1971), was added during the Vietnam War. With so many teenage men volunteering for or drafted into military service, and with so many young people protesting against American political decisions, public opinion favored giving them the opportunity to play a role in the political process by voting. The Twenty-sixth Amendment lowered the voting age to 18.

The Debate Over Original Intent

Obviously the Constitution has changed considerably over the past two centuries. But as new amendments are added and the president, Congress, and the Supreme Court reinterpret the Constitution, the question arises over how much weight should be placed on the "original intent" of the framers of the Constitution. Conservatives object to the judicial activism of federal judges, who try to mold the Constitution to meet modern demands. Senator Barry Goldwater, in his 1960 book *The Conscience of a Conservative*, warned that the framers had designed a Constitution to *limit* the powers of the federal government because they believed that a powerful state would thwart human liberty. "The Constitution is what its authors intended it to be and said it was—not what the Supreme Court says it is," Goldwater insisted.

On the eve of the Constitution's bicentennial, Attorney General Edwin Meese revived Senator Goldwater's argument. Supreme Court decisions were not the "supreme law of the land," said the attorney general, adding that each of the three branches of the government had an equal duty to interpret the Constitution. Meese criticized judges who read their own values into the Constitution, rather than follow the "original intent" of the framers. A liberal

Attorney General Edwin Meese III (center) speaks with President Ronald Reagan during a staff meeting at the White House. Meese once voiced the opinion that each of the three branches of government had an equal duty to interpret the Constitution and that Supreme Court justices should not read their own values into the document.

Supreme Court justice, William Brennan, responded that the historical sources on the Constitutional Convention were too brief and ambiguous to give us complete assurance about the framers' intentions. And because the delegates often disagreed on issues, there remained the question of *whose* intent to follow. Brennan argued that the Constitution must not be judged in terms of "a world dead and gone," but that judges must apply the Constitution's basic principles to modern problems.

James Madison himself argued against trying to judge the Constitution by the arguments of the delegates at the Constitutional Convention. The author of the best notes on the convention, he kept them secret until his death a half century later. Madison believed that the Constitution should be interpreted according to its popular understanding at the time of ratification. However, there is little historical data on the contemporary public's interpretation of the document.

Supreme Court Justice William Brennan believes that the Constitution should not be judged in terms of "a world dead and gone" but that judges should apply the Constitution's basic principles to contemporary problems.

Reformers in American history have not limited their vision to the original intent of the framers. Thomas Jefferson warned that people should not "look at constitutions with sanctimonious reverence, and deem them like of the ark of the covenant, too sacred to be touched." Jefferson did not advocate frequent change to the Constitution, but agreed that "laws and institutions must go hand in hand with the progress of the human mind." A century later, Woodrow Wilson declared that the meaning of the Constitution should be determined "not by the original intentions of those who drew the paper, but by the . . . new aspects of life itself." President Harry Truman commented that "a constitution that is not adaptable—that prevents the government from acting for the general welfare of the people—will not survive."

Judge Robert Bork, nominated by President Ronald Reagan to be an associate justice of the Supreme Court, answers questions during his confirmation hearing before the Senate Judiciary Committee in 1987. By a vote of 58 to 42, the Senate rejected Bork's nomination.

SEVEN

Toward the Third Century

As the United States entered its third century of self-government, it witnessed some troublesome constitutional problems. During the bicentennial year of the Constitution, for the 27th time in its history, the Senate rejected a nominee for the Supreme Court. This high rate of rejection contrasted with the very few times that the Senate had refused to confirm a Cabinet officer. Senators have generally believed that presidents had the right to choose their own cabinets. But the Supreme Court is an independent branch of the government, whose appointments must satisfy the legislative as well as the executive branch, for the decisions of the Court affected not only the rights of all citizens but the policies of the government.

Also in the bicentennial year, a joint Senate and House committee investigated the Iran-Contra scandal. Testifying before the committee, administration officials talked as if foreign policy were solely the president's responsibility. Citing the need for presidential leadership in foreign affairs, as well as the need for secrecy to protect policy initiatives, some witnesses admitted to having withheld important information and even lying to Congress about arms shipments to Iran and diversion of funds to the Nicaraguan Contra forces. Such behavior ran contrary to the idea of a government of checks and balances.

War powers became an area of increasing disagreement between Congress and the presidency. The Constitution specified numerous functions for Congress in military matters, while designating the president as commander in chief. Congress has the sole right to declare war. It has exercised this right only five times, even though the United States has been involved in additional conflicts. After presidents sent American troops into wars in Korea and

97

Vietnam without asking for congressional declarations of war, Congress responded by passing the War Powers Act in 1973. This law requires the president to notify Congress when troops are sent into combat overseas and gives Congress the authority to withdraw those troops after 60 days. Despite the War Powers Act, President Reagan sent American military forces into Grenada, Libya, and the Persian Gulf without congressional sanction. Constitutional scholar Edwin Corwin has called the Constitution's vagueness on foreign policy-making "an invitation to struggle" between Congress and the presidency. Clearly that struggle will continue into America's third century.

The right to privacy also looms as an increasingly controversial constitutional issue. Citing women's right to privacy, the Supreme Court struck down state laws banning abortion in the case of *Roe v. Wade* in 1972. Furthermore, questions of privacy have become involved in such issues as wiretapping of

A "pro-life" demonstrator (left) and a "pro-choice" demonstrator (right) confront each other during a 1984 antiabortion rally in Boston, Massachusetts. In 1972, the Supreme Court declared state laws banning abortion to be an unconstitutional violation of the right of privacy; however, this issue continues to be controversial.

98

telephones and computer surveillance. At first the Supreme Court ruled wiretapping legal because no property was broken into and entered. But in 1967, the Court overturned its earlier rulings and banned wiretaps without warrants on the ground that "the Fourth Amendment protects people, not places." By the 1980s, advanced computer technology permitted the collection of vast amounts of personal information on individuals, covering everything from their finances to their health records, traffic tickets, and business dealings. Such data banks raise issues of privacy that the framers of the Constitution could scarcely have anticipated. Congress and the courts must grapple with these issues in the future.

Minority rights will also continue to be constitutional issues in the nation's third century. A national consensus has developed behind civil rights legislation that outlawed discrimination in hiring, wages, and promotions. But no such agreement extends to "affirmative action." Is it permissible for the federal and state governments to offer preferential treatment to minority groups for jobs and promotions, to help end past patterns of discrimination? Or are such affirmative action plans simply "reverse discrimination" against the majority? The Supreme Court has decided a number of affirmative action cases, but the larger issue remains open.

Failure of the Equal Rights Amendment (ERA), which fell three states short of the two-thirds of the states needed for ratification, left unanswered the Constitution's protection of women's rights. The fight for the ERA spawned large, active organizations both for and against, which will undoubtedly continue their dispute into the future. Even without the Equal Rights Amendment, Congress and the Supreme Court will face numerous issues relating to women's salaries and promotions, maternity leave, and private clubs that ban women members.

These unresolved issues and continued disputes and debates are signs not of the weakness of the Constitution of the United States but of its strength. While setting definite limits on government activities and protecting individual rights, the Constitution leaves room for government to grow and for rights to be extended into areas that may not have been thought of, or may not even have existed, when the Constitution was drafted. The division of power and checks and balances among the branches of government may frustrate a president with a bold program of action or a Congress that sees its favored bills vetoed or declared unconstitutional. But whatever the frustrations, the limitations, or even the injustices of the moment, the Constitution continues to provide the framework of a democratic government for "we the people of the United States" to tackle the issues before us.

Constitution of the
United States of America

We the People of the United States, in Order to form a more perfect Union, establish Justice, insure domestic Tranquility, provide for the common defence, promote the general Welfare, and secure the Blessings of Liberty to ourselves and our Posterity, do ordain and establish this Constitution for the United States of America.

ARTICLE I

Section 1. All legislative Powers herein granted shall be vested in a Congress of the United States, which shall consist of a Senate and House of Representatives.

Section 2. The House of Representatives shall be composed of Members chosen every second Year by the People of the several States, and the Electors in each State shall have the Qualifications requisite for Electors of the most numerous Branch of the State Legislature.

No Person shall be a Representative who shall not have attained to the Age of twenty five Years, and been seven Years a Citizen of the United States, and who shall not, when elected, be an Inhabitant of that State in which he shall be chosen.

Representatives and direct Taxes shall be apportioned among the several States which may be included within this Union, according to their respective Numbers, which shall be determined by adding to the whole Number of free Persons, including those bound to Service for a Term of Years, and excluding Indians not taxed, three fifths of all other persons. The actual Enumeration shall be made within three Years after the first Meeting of the Congress of the United States, and within every subsequent Term of ten Years, in such Manner as they shall by Law direct. The Number of Representatives shall not exceed one for every thirty Thousand, but each State shall have at Least one Representative; and until such enumeration shall be made, the State of New Hampshire shall be entitled to chuse three, Massachusetts eight, Rhode-Island and Providence Plantations one, Connecticut five, New-York six, New Jersey four, Pennsylvania eight, Delaware one, Maryland six, Virginia ten, North Carolina five, South Carolina five, and Georgia three.

When vacancies happen in the Representation from any State, the Executive Authority thereof shall issue Writs of Election to fill such Vacancies.

The House of Representatives shall chuse their Speaker and other Officers; and shall have the sole Power of Impeachment.

Section 3. The Senate of the United States shall be composed of two Senators from each State, chosen by the Legislature thereof, for six Years; and each Senator shall have one Vote.

Immediately after they shall be assembled in Consequence of the first Election, they shall be divided as equally as may be into three Classes. The Seats of the Senators of the first Class shall be vacated at the Expiration of the Second Year, of the second Class at the Expiration of the fourth Year, and of the third Class at the Expiration of the sixth Year; so that one-third may be chosen every second Year; and if Vacancies happen by Resignation, or otherwise, during the Recess of the Legislature of any State, the Executive thereof may make temporary Appointments until the next Meeting of the Legislature, which shall then fill such Vacancies.

No Person shall be a Senator who shall not have attained to the Age of thirty Years, and been nine Years a Citizen of the United States, and who shall not, when elected, be an Inhabitant of that State for which he shall be chosen.

The Vice President of the United States shall be President of the Senate, but shall have no Vote, unless they be equally divided.

The Senate shall chuse their other Officers, and also a President pro tempore, in the absence of the Vice President, or when he shall exercise the Office of President of the United States.

100

The Senate shall have the sole Power to try all Impeachments. When sitting for that Purpose, they shall be on Oath or Affirmation. When the President of the United States is tried, the Chief Justice shall preside: And no Person shall be convicted without the Concurrence of two-thirds of the Members present.

Judgment in Cases of Impeachment shall not extend further than to removal from Office, and disqualification to hold and enjoy any Office of honor, Trust, or Profit under the United States: but the Party convicted shall nevertheless be liable and subject to Indictment, Trial, Judgment, and Punishment, according to Law.

Section 4. The Time, Places and Manner of holding Elections for Senators and Representatives, shall be prescribed in each State by the Legislature thereof; but the Congress may at any time by Law make or alter such Regulations, except as to the Places of chusing Senators.

The Congress shall assemble at least once in every Year, and such Meeting shall be on the first Monday in December, unless they shall by Law appoint a different Day.

Section 5. Each House shall be the Judge of the Elections, Returns, and Qualifications of its own Members, and a Majority of each shall constitute a Quorum to do Business; but a smaller Number may adjourn from day to day, and may be authorized to compel the Attendance of absent Members, in such Manner, and under such Penalties as each House may provide.

Each House may determine the Rules of its Proceedings, punish its Members for disorderly Behavior, and, with the Concurrence of two thirds, expel a Member.

Each House shall keep a Journal of its Proceedings, and from time to time publish the same, excepting such Parts as may in their Judgment require Secrecy; and the Yeas and Nays of the Members of either House on any question shall, at the Desire of one fifth of those Present be entered on the Journal.

Neither House, during the Session of Congress, shall, without the Consent of the other, adjourn for more than three days, nor to any other Place than that in which the two Houses shall be sitting.

Section 6. The Senators and Representatives shall receive a Compensation for their Services, to be ascertained by Law, and paid out of the Treasury of the United States. They shall in all Cases, except Treason, Felony and Breach of the Peace, be privileged from Arrest during their Attendance at the Session of their respective Houses, and in going to and returning from the same; and for any Speech or Debate in either House, they shall not be questioned in any other Place.

No Senator or Representative shall, during the Time for which he was elected, be appointed to any civil Office under the Authority of the United States, which shall have been created, or the Emoluments whereof shall have been encreased during such time; and no Person holding any Office under the United States, shall be a Member of either House during his Continuance in Office.

Section 7. All Bills for raising Revenue shall originate in the House of Representatives; but the Senate may propose or concur with Amendments as on other Bills.

Every Bill which shall have passed the House of Representatives and the Senate, shall, before it become a Law, be presented to the President of the United States; if he approve he shall sign it, but if not he shall return it, with his Objections to that House in which it shall have originated, who shall enter the Objections at large on their Journal, and proceed to reconsider it. If after such Reconsideration two thirds of that House shall agree to pass the Bill, it shall be sent, together with the Objections, to the other House, by which it shall likewise be reconsidered, and if approved by two thirds of that House, it shall become a Law. But in all such Cases the Votes of both Houses shall be determined by Yeas and Nays, and the Names of the Persons voting for and against the Bill shall be entered on the Journal of each House respectively. If any Bill shall not be returned by the President within ten Days (Sundays excepted) after it shall have been presented to him, the Same shall be a Law, in like Manner as if he had signed it, unless the Congress by their Adjournment prevent its Return, in which Case it shall not be a Law.

Every Order, Resolution, or Vote to which the Concurrence of the Senate and House of Representatives may be necessary (except on a question of Adjournment) shall be presented to the President of the United States; and before the Same shall take Effect, shall be approved by him, or being disapproved by him, shall be repassed by two thirds of the Senate and House of Representatives, according to the Rules and Limitations prescribed in the Case of a Bill.

Section 8. The Congress shall have Power To lay and collect Taxes, Duties, Imposts and Excises, to pay the Debts and provide for the common Defence and general Welfare of the United States; but all Duties, Imposts and Excises shall be uniform throughout the United States;

To borrow money on the credit of the United States;

To regulate Commerce with foreign Nations, and among the several States, and with the Indian Tribes;

To establish an uniform Rule of Naturalization, and uniform Laws on the subject of Bankruptcies throughout the United States;

To coin Money, regulate the Value thereof, and of foreign Coin, and fix the Standard of Weights and Measures;

To provide for the Punishment of counterfeiting the Securities and current Coin of the United States;

To establish Post Offices and post Roads;

To promote the Progress of Science and useful Arts, by securing for limited Times to Authors and Inventors the exclusive Right to their respective Writings and Discoveries;

To constitute Tribunals inferior to the supreme Court;

To define and punish Piracies and Felonies committed on the high Seas, and Offenses against the Law of Nations;

To declare War, grant Letters of Marque and Reprisal and make Rules concerning Captures on Land and Water;

To raise and support Armies, but no Appropriation of Money to that Use shall be for a longer Term than two Years;

To provide and maintain a Navy;

To make Rules for the Government and Regulation of the land and naval Forces;

To provide for calling forth the Militia to execute the Laws of the Union, suppress Insurrections and repel Invasions;

To provide for organizing, arming, and disciplining the Militia, and for governing such Part of them as may be employed in the Service of the United States, reserving to the States respectively, the Appointment of the Officers, and the Authority of training the Militia according to the discipline prescribed by Congress;

To exercise exclusive Legislation in all Cases whatsoever, over such District (not exceeding ten Miles square) as may, by Cession of particular States, and the acceptance of Congress, become the Seat of the Government of the United States, and to exercise like Authority over all Places purchased by the Consent of the Legislature of the State in which the Same shall be, for the Erection of Forts, Magazines, Arsenals, dock-Yards, and other needful Buildings;—And

To make all Laws which shall be necessary and proper for carrying into Execution the foregoing Powers, and all other Powers vested by this Constitution in the Government of the United States, or in any Department or Officer thereof.

Section 9. The Migration or Importation of Such Persons as any of the States now existing shall think proper to admit, shall not be prohibited by the Congress prior to the Year one thousand eight hundred and eight, but a tax or duty may be imposed on such Importation, not exceeding ten dollars for each Person.

The privilege of the Writ of Habeas Corpus shall not be suspended, unless when in Cases of Rebellion or Invasion the public Safety may require it.

No Bill of Attainder or ex post facto Law shall be passed.

No capitation, or other direct, Tax shall be laid, unless in Proportion to the Census or Enumeration herein before directed to be taken.

No Tax or Duty shall be laid on Articles exported from any State.

No preference shall be given by any Regulation of Commerce or Revenue to the Ports of one State over those of another: nor shall Vessels bound to, or from, one State be obliged to enter, clear, or pay Duties in another.

No money shall be drawn from the Treasury, but in Consequence of Appropriations made by Law; and a regular Statement and Account of the Receipts and Expenditures of all public Money shall be published from time to time.

No Title of Nobility shall be granted by the United States: And no Person holding any Office of Profit or Trust under them, shall, without the Consent of the Congress, accept of any present, Emolument, Office, or Title, of any kind whatever, from any King, Prince, or foreign State.

Section 10. No State shall enter into any Treaty, Alliance, or Confederation; grant Letters of Marque and Reprisal; coin Money; emit Bills of Credit; make any Thing but gold and silver Coin a Tender in Payment of Debts; pass any

Bill of Attainder, ex post facto Law, or Law impairing the Obligation of Contracts, or grant any Title of Nobility.

No State shall, without the Consent of the Congress, lay any Imposts or Duties on Imports or Exports, except what may be absolutely necessary for executing its inspection Laws: and the net Produce of all Duties and Imposts, laid by any State on Imports or Exports, shall be for the Use of the Treasury of the United States; and all such Laws shall be subject to the Revision and Control of the Congress.

No State shall, without the Consent of Congress, lay any duty of Tonnage, keep Troops, or Ships of War in time of Peace, enter into any Agreement or Compact with another State, or with a foreign Power, or engage in War, unless actually invaded, or in such imminent Danger as will not admit of delay.

ARTICLE II

Section 1. The executive Power shall be vested in a President of the United States of America. He shall hold his Office during the Term of four years, and, together with the Vice President, chosen for the same Term, be elected, as follows:

Each State shall appoint, in such Manner as the Legislature thereof may direct, a Number of Electors, equal to the whole Number of Senators and Representatives to which the State may be entitled in the Congress: but no Senator or Representative, or Person holding an Office of Trust or Profit under the United States, shall be appointed an Elector.

The Electors shall meet in their respective States, and vote by Ballot for two persons, of whom one at least shall not be an Inhabitant of the same State with themselves. And they shall make a List of all the Persons voted for, and of the Number of Votes for each; which List they shall sign and certify, and transmit sealed to the Seat of the Government of the United States, directed

103

to the President of the Senate. The President of the Senate shall, in the Presence of the Senate and House of Representatives, open all the Certificates, and the Votes shall then be counted. The Person having the greatest Number of Votes shall be the President, if such Number be a Majority of the whole Number of Electors appointed; and if there be more than one who have such Majority, and have an equal Number of Votes, then the House of Representatives shall immediately chuse by Ballot one of them for President; and if no Person have a majority, then from the five highest on the List the said House shall in like Manner chuse the President. But in chusing the President, the Votes shall be taken by States, the Representation from each State having one Vote; A quorum for this Purpose shall consist of a Member or Members from two thirds of the States, and a Majority of all the States shall be necessary to a Choice. In every Case, after the Choice of the President, the Person having the greatest Number of Votes of the Electors shall be the Vice President. But if there should remain two or more who have equal Votes, the Senate shall chuse from them by Ballot the Vice President.

The Congress may determine the Time of chusing the Electors, and the Day on which they shall give their Votes; which Day shall be the same throughout the United States.

No person except a natural born Citizen, or a Citizen of the United States, at the time of the Adoption of this Constitution, shall be eligible to the Office of President; neither shall any Person be eligible to that Office who shall not have attained to the Age of thirty five Years, and been fourteen Years a Resident within the United States.

In case of the Removal of the President from Office, or of his Death, resignation, or Inability to discharge the Powers and Duties of the said Office, the same shall devolve on the Vice President, and the Congress may by Law provide for the Case of Removal, Death, Resignation or Inability, both of the President and Vice President, declaring what Officer shall then act as President, and such Officer shall act accordingly, until the Disability be removed, or a President shall be elected.

The President shall, at stated Times, receive for his Services, a Compensation, which shall neither be encreased not diminished during the Period for which he shall have been elected, and he shall not receive within that Period any other Emolument from the United States, or any of them.

Before he enter on the Execution of his Office, he shall take the following Oath or Affirmation:—"I do solemnly swear (or affirm) that I will faithfully execute the Office of President of the United States, and will to the best of my Ability, preserve, protect and defend the Constitution of the United States."

Section 2. The President shall be Commander in Chief of the Army and Navy of the United States, and of the Militia of the several States, when called into the actual Service of the United States; he may require the Opinion, in writing, of the principal Officer in each of the executive Departments, upon any subject relating to the Duties of their respective Offices, and he shall have Power to grant Reprieves and Pardons for Offenses against the United States, except in Cases of Impeachment.

He shall have Power, by and with the Advice and Consent of the Senate, to make Treaties, provided two thirds of the Senators present concur; and he shall nominate, and by and with the Advice and Consent of the Senate, shall appoint Ambassadors, other public Ministers and Consuls, Judges of the supreme Court, and all other Officers of the United States, whose Appointments are not herein otherwise provided for, and which shall be established by law; but the Congress may by Law vest the Appointment of such inferior Officers, as they think proper, in the President alone, in the Courts of Law, or in the Heads of Departments.

The President shall have Power to fill up all Vacancies that may happen during the Recess of the Senate, by granting Commissions which shall expire at the End of their next Session.

Section 3. He shall from time to time give to the Congress Information of the State of the Union, and recommend to their Consideration such Measures as he shall judge necessary and expedient; he may, on extraordinary Occasions, convene both Houses, or either of them, and in Case of Disagreement between them, with Respect to the Time of Adjournment, he may adjourn them to such Time as he shall think proper; he shall receive Ambassadors and other public Ministers; he shall take Care that the Laws be faithfully executed, and shall Commission all the Officers of the United States.

Section 4. The President, Vice President and all civil Officers of the United States, shall be removed from Office on Impeachment for, and Conviction of, Treason, Bribery, or other high Crimes and Misdemeanors.

ARTICLE III

Section 1. The judicial Power of the United States, shall be vested in one supreme Court, and in such inferior Courts as the Congress may from time to time ordain and establish. The Judges, both of the supreme and inferior Courts, shall hold their offices during good Behaviour, and shall, at stated Times, receive for their Services a Compensation which shall not be diminished during their Continuance in Office.

Section 2. The judicial Power shall extend to all Cases, in Law and Equity, arising under this constitution, the Laws of the United States, and Treaties made, or which shall be made, under their Authority;—to all Cases affecting Ambas-

sadors, other public Ministers and Consuls; to all Cases of admiralty and maritime Jurisdiction;—to Controversies to which the United States shall be a Party;—to Controversies between two or more States;—between a State and Citizens of another State;—between Citizens of different States;—between Citizens of the same State claiming Lands under Grants of different States, and between a State, or the Citizens thereof, and foreign States, Citizens or Subjects.

In all Cases affecting Ambassadors, other public Ministers and consuls, and those in which a State shall be Party, the supreme Court shall have original Jurisdiction. In all the other Cases before mentioned, the supreme Court shall have appellate Jurisdiction, both as to Law and Fact, with such Exceptions, and under such Regulations as the Congress shall make.

The trial of all Crimes, except in Cases of Impeachment, shall be by Jury; and such Trial shall be held in the State where the said Crimes shall have been committed; but when not committed within any State, the Trial shall be at such Place or Places as the Congress may by Law have directed.

Section 3. Treason against the United States, shall consist only in levying War against them, or in adhering to their Enemies, giving them Aid and Comfort. No Person shall be convicted of Treason unless on the Testimony of two Witnesses to the same overt Act, or on Confession in open Court.

The Congress shall have power to declare the Punishment of Treason, but no Attainder of Treason shall work Corruption of Blood, or Forfeiture except during the Life of the Person attained.

ARTICLE IV

Section 1. Full Faith and Credit shall be given in each State to the public Acts, Records, and judicial Proceedings of every other State. And the Congress may by general Laws prescribe the Manner in which such Acts, Records and Proceedings shall be proved, and the Effect thereof.

Section 2. The Citizens of each State shall be entitled to all Privileges and Immunities of Citizens in the several States.

A Person charged in any State with Treason, Felony, or other Crime, who shall flee from Justice, and be found in another State, shall on demand of the executive authority of the State from which he fled, be delivered up, to be removed to the State having Jurisdiction of the Crime.

No Person held to Service or Labour in one State, under the Laws thereof, escaping into another, shall, in Consequence of any Law or Regulation therein, be discharged from such Service or Labour, but shall be delivered up on Claim of the Party to whom such Service or Labour may be due.

Section 3. New States may be admitted by the Congress into this Union; but no new State shall be formed or erected within the Jurisdiction of any other state; nor any State be formed by the Junction of two or more States, or parts of States, without the Consent of the Legislatures of the States concerned as well as of Congress.

The Congress shall have Power to dispose of and make all needful Rules and Regulations respecting the Territory of other Property belonging to the United States; and nothing in this Constitution shall be so construed as to Prejudice any Claims of the United States, or of any particular State.

Section 4. The United States shall guarantee to every State in this Union a Republican Form of Government, and shall protect each of them against Invasion; and on Application of the Legislature, or of the Executive (when the Legislature cannot be convened) against domestic Violence.

The Congress, whenever two thirds of both Houses shall deem it necessary, shall propose Amendments to this Constitution, or, on the Application of the Legislatures of two thirds of the several States, shall call a Convention for proposing Amendments, which, in either Case, shall be valid to all Intents and Purposes, as part of this Constitution, when ratified by the Legislatures of three fourths of the several States, or by Conventions in three fourths thereof, as the one or the other Mode of ratification may be proposed by the Congress; Provided that no Amendment which may be made prior to the Year One thousand eight hundred and eight shall in any Manner affect the first and fourth Clauses in the Ninth Section of the first Article, and that no State without its Consent, shall be deprived of its equal Suffrage in the Senate.

All Debts contracted and Engagements entered into, before the Adoption of this Constitution shall be as valid against the United States under this Constitution, as under the Confederation.

This Constitution, and the Laws of the United States which shall be made in Pursuance thereof, and all Treaties made, or which shall be made, under Authority of the United States, shall be the supreme Law of the Land, and the Judges in every State shall be bound thereby, any Thing in the Constitution or Laws of any State to the Contrary notwithstanding.

The Senators and Representatives before mentioned, and the Members of the several State Legislatures, and all executive and judicial Officers, both of the United States and of the several States, shall be bound by Oath or Affirmation, to support this constitution; but no religious Test shall ever be required as a Qualification to any Office or public Trust under the United States.

ARTICLE VII

The Ratification of the Conventions of nine States shall be sufficient for the Establishment of this Constitution between the States so ratifying the Same.

DONE in Convention by the Unanimous Consent of the States present the Seventeenth Day of September in the Year of our Lord one thousand seven hundred and Eighty seven and of the Independence of the United States of America the Twelfth. IN WITNESS whereof We have here unto subscribed our Names,

GO. WASHINGTON
Presidt. and deputy from Virginia

NEW HAMPSHIRE
John Langdon,   Nicholas Gilman.

MASSACHUSETTS
Nathaniel Gorhan,   Rufus King.

CONNECTICUT
Wm. Saml. Johnson,   Roger Sherman.

NEW YORK
Alexander Hamilton.

NEW JERSEY
Wil: Livingston,   Wm. Paterson,
David Brearley,   Jona. Dayton.

PENNSYLVANIA
B. Franklin   Thomas Mifflin,
Robt. Morris,   Geo: Clymer,
Tho: Fitzsimons,   Jared Ingersoll,
James Wilson,   Gouv: Morris.

DELAWARE
Geo: Read,   Gunning Bedford,
John Dickinson,   Jun'r,
Jaco: Broom,   Richard Bassett.

MARYLAND
James M'Henry,   Dan: of St. Thos.
Danl Carroll,   Jenifer.

VIRGINIA
John Blair   James Madison, Jr.

NORTH CAROLINA
Wm. Blount   Rich'd Dobbs
Hu. Williamson,   Spaight.

SOUTH CAROLINA
J. Rutledge,   Charles Cotesworth
                       Pinckney,
Charles Pinckney, Pierce Butler.

GEORGIA
William Few,   Abr. Baldwin.
Attest: Wm. Jackson, Sectry.

Articles in addition to, and amendment of, the Constitution of the United States of America, proposed by Congress, and ratified by the legislatures of the several states, pursuant to the fifth article of the original Constitution.

AMENDMENT I

Congress shall make no law respecting an establishment of religion, or prohibiting the free exercise thereof; or abridging the freedom of speech, or of the press; or the right of the people peaceably to assemble, and to petition the Government for a redress of grievances.

AMENDMENT II

A well regulated Militia, being necessary to the security of a free State, the right of the people to keep and bear Arms, shall not be infringed.

AMENDMENT III

No Soldier shall, in time of peace be quartered in any house, without the consent of the Owner, nor in time of war, but in a manner to be prescribed by law.

AMENDMENT IV

The right of the people to be secure in their persons, houses, papers, and effects, against unreasonable searches and seizures, shall not be violated, and no Warrants shall issue, but upon probable cause, supported by Oath or affirmation, and particularly describing the place to be searched, and the persons or things to be seized.

AMENDMENT V

No person shall be held to answer for a capital, or otherwise infamous crime, unless on a presentment or indictment of a Grand Jury, except in cases arising in the land or naval forces, or in the Militia, when in actual service in time of War or public danger; nor shall any person be subject for the same offenses to be twice put in jeopardy of life or limb; nor shall be compelled in any criminal case to be a witness against himself, nor be deprived of life, liberty, or property, without due process of law; nor shall private property be taken for public use, without just compensation.

AMENDMENT VI

In all criminal prosecutions, the accused shall enjoy the right to a speedy and public trial, by an impartial jury of the State and district wherein the crime shall have been committed, which district shall have been previously ascertained by law, and to be informed of the nature and cause of the accusation; to be confronted with the witnesses against him; to have compulsory process for obtaining witnesses in his favor, and to have the Assistance of Counsel for his defence.

AMENDMENT VII

In Suits at common law, where the value in controversy shall exceed twenty dollars, the right of trial by jury shall be preserved, and no fact tried by a jury, shall be otherwise reexamined in any Court of the United States, than according to the rules of the common law.

AMENDMENT VII

Excessive bail shall not be required, nor excessive fines imposed, nor cruel and unusual punishments inflicted.

AMENDMENT IX

The enumeration in the Constitution, of certain rights, shall not be construed to deny or disparage others retained by the people.

AMENDMENT X

The powers not delegated to the United States by the Constitution, nor prohibited by it to the States, are reserved to the States respectively, or to the people.

AMENDMENT XI

The Judicial power of the United States shall not be construed to extend to any suit in law or equity, commenced or prosecuted against one of the United States by Citizens of another State, or by Citizens or Subjects of any Foreign State.

AMENDMENT XII

The Electors shall meet in their respective states and vote by ballot for President and Vice-President, one of whom, at least, shall not be an inhabitant of the same state with themselves; they shall name in their ballots the person voted for, as President, and in distinct ballots the person voted for as Vice-President, and they shall make distinct lists of all persons voted for as President, and of all persons voted for as Vice-President, and of the number of votes for each, which lists they shall sign and certify, and transmit sealed to the seat of the government of the United States, directed to the President of the Senate;—The President of the Senate shall, in the presence of the Senate and House of Representatives, open all the certificates and the votes shall then be counted;—The person having the greatest number of votes for President, shall be the President, if such number be a majority of the whole number of Electors appointed; and if no person have such majority, then from the persons having the highest numbers not exceeding three on the list of those voted for as President, the House of Representatives shall choose immediately, by ballot, the President. But in choosing the President, the votes shall be taken by states the representatation from each state having one vote; a quorum for this purpose shall consist of a member or members from two-thirds of the states, and a majority of all the states shall be necessary to a choice. And if the House of Representatives shall not choose a President whenever the right of choice shall devolve upon them, before the fourth day of March next following, then the Vice-President shall act as President, as in the case of the death or other constitutional disability of the President.—The person having the greatest number of votes as Vice-President, shall be the Vice-President, if such number be a majority of the whole number of Electors appointed, and if no person have a majority, then from the two highest numbers on the list, the Senate shall choose the Vice-President; a quorum for the purpose shall consist of two-thirds of the whole number of Senators, and a majority of the whole number shall be necessary to a choice. But no person constitutionally ineligible to the office of President shall be eligible to that of Vice-President of the United States.

AMENDMENT XIII

Section 1. Neither slavery nor involuntary servitude, except as a punishment for crime whereof the party shall have been duly convicted, shall exist within the United States, or any place subject to their jurisdiction.

Section 2. Congress shall have power to enforce this article by appropriate legislation.

AMENDMENT XIV

Section 1. All persons born or naturalized in the United States, and subject to the jurisdiction thereof, are citizens of the United States and of the State wherein they reside. No State shall make or enforce any law which shall abridge the privileges or immunities of citizens of the United States; nor shall any State deprive any person of life, liberty, or property without due process of law, nor deny to any person within its jurisdiction the equal protection of the laws.

Section 2. Representatives shall be apportioned among the several States according to their respective numbers, counting the whole number of persons in each State, excluding Indians not taxed. But when the right to vote at any election for the choice of electors for President and Vice-President of the United States, Representatives in Congress, the Executive and Judicial officers of a State, or the members of the Legislature thereof, is denied to any of the male inhabitants of such State, being twenty-one years of age, and citizens of the United States, or in any way abridged, except for participation in rebellion, or other crime, the basis of representation therein shall be reduced in the proportion which the number of such male citizens shall bear to the whole number of male citizens twenty-one years of age in such State.

Section 3. No person shall be a Senator or Representative in Congress, or elector of President and Vice-President, or hold any office, civil or military, under the United States, or under any State, who, having previously taken an oath, as a member of Congress, or as an officer of the United States, or as a member of any State legislature, or as an executive or judicial officer of any State, to support the Constitution of the United States, shall have engaged in insurrection or rebellion against the same, or given aid or comfort to the enemies thereof. But Congress may by a vote of two-thirds of each House, remove such disability.

Section 4. The validity of the public debt of the United States, authorized by law, including debts incurred for payment of pensions and bounties for services in suppressing insurrection or rebellion, shall not be questioned. But neither the United States nor any State shall assume or pay any debt or obligation incurred in aid of insurrection or rebellion against the United States, or any claim for the loss or emancipation of any slave; but all such debts, obligations and claims shall be held illegal and void.

Section 5. The Congress shall have power to enforce, by appropriate legislation, the provisions of this article.

AMENDMENT XV

Section 1. The right of citizens of the United States to vote shall not be denied or abridged by the United States or by any State on account of race, color, or previous condition of servitude.

Section 2. The Congress shall have power to enforce this article by appropriate legislation.

AMENDMENT XVI

The Congress shall have power to lay and collect taxes on incomes, from whatever source derived, without apportionment among the several States, and without regard to any census or enumeration.

AMENDMENT XVII

The Senate of the United States shall be composed of two Senators from each State, elected by the people thereof, for six years; and each Senator shall have one vote. The electors in each State shall have the qualifications requisite for electors of the most numerous branch of the State legislatures.

When vacancies happen in the representation of any State in the Senate, the executive authority of such State shall issue writs of election to fill such vacancies: *Provided*, That the legislature of any State may empower the executive thereof to make temporary appointments until the people fill the vacancies by election as the legislature may direct. This amendment shall not be so construed as to affect the election or term of any Senator chosen before it becomes valid as part of the Constitution.

Section 1. After one year from the ratification of this article the manufacture, sale, or transportation of intoxicating liquors within, the importation thereof into, or the exportation thereof from the United States and all territory subject to the jurisdiction thereof for beverage purposes is hereby prohibited.

Section 2. The Congress and the several States shall have concurrent power to enforce this article by appropriate legislation.

Section 3. This article shall be inoperative unless it shall have been ratified as an amendment to the Constitution by the legislatures of the several States, as provided in the Constitution, within seven years from the date of the submission hereof to the States by the Congress.

AMENDMENT XIX

The right of citizens of the United States to vote shall not be denied or abridged by the United States or by any State on account of sex.

Congress shall have power to enforce this article by appropriate legislation.

AMENDMENT XX

Section 1. The terms of the President and Vice-President shall end at noon on the 20th day of January, and the terms of Senators and Representatives at noon on the 3d day of January, of the years in which such terms would have ended if this article had not been ratified; and the terms of their successors shall then begin.

Section 2. The Congress shall assemble at least once in every year, and such meeting shall begin at noon on the 3d day of January, unless they by law appoint a different day.

Section 3. If, at the time fixed for the beginning of the term of the President, the President elect shall have died, the Vice-President elect shall become President. If a President shall not have been chosen before the time fixed for the beginning of his term, or if the President elect shall have failed to qualify, then the Vice-President elect shall act as President until a President shall have qualified; and the Congress may by law provide for the case wherein neither a President elect nor a Vice-President elect shall have qualified, declaring who shall then act as President, or the manner in which one who is to act shall be selected, and such person shall act accordingly until a President or Vice-President shall have qualified.

Section 4. The Congress may by law provide for the case of the death of any of the persons from whom the House of Representatives may choose a President whenever the right of choice shall have devolved upon them, and for the case of the death of any of the persons from whom the Senate may choose a Vice-President whenever the right of choice shall have devolved upon them.

Section 5. Sections 1 and 2 shall take effect on the 15th day of October following the ratification of this article.

Section 6. This article shall be inoperative unless it shall have been ratified as an amendment to the Constitution by the legislatures of three-fourths of the several States within seven years from the date of its submission.

AMENDMENT XXI

Section 1. The eighteenth article of amendment to the Constitution of the United States is hereby repealed.

Section 2. The transportation or importation into any State, Territory, or possession of the United States for delivery or use therein of intoxicating liquors, in violation of the laws thereof, is hereby prohibited.

Section 3. This article shall be inoperative unless it shall have been ratified as an amendment to the Constitution by conventions in the several States, as provided in the Constitution, within seven years from the date of the submission hereof to the States by the Congress.

Section 1. No person shall be elected to the office of the President more than twice, and no person who has held the office of President, or acted as President, for more than two years of a term to which some other person was elected President shall be elected to the office of the President more than once. But this Article shall not apply to any person holding the office of President when this Article was proposed by the Congress, and shall not prevent any person who may be holding the office of President, or acting as President, during the term within which this Article becomes operative, from holding the office of President or acting as President during the remainder of such term.

Section 2. This article shall be inoperative unless it shall have been ratified as an amendment to the Constitution by the legislatures of three-fourths of the several States within seven years from the date of its submission to the States by the Congress.

Section 1. The District constituting the seat of Government of the United States shall appoint in such manner as the Congress may direct:

A number of electors of President and Vice President equal to the whole number of Senators and Representatives in Congress to which the District would be entitled if it were a State, but in no event more than the least populous State; they shall be in addition to those appointed by the States, but they shall be considered, for the purposes of the election of President and Vice President, to be electors appointed by a State; and they shall meet in the district and perform such duties as provided by the twelfth article of amendment.

Section 2. The Congress shall have power to enforce this article by appropriate legislation.

Section 1. The right of citizens of the United States to vote in any primary or other election for President or Vice President, for electors for President or Vice President, or for Senator or Representative in Congress, shall not be denied or abridged by the United States or any State by reason of failure to pay any poll tax or other tax.

Section 2. The Congress shall have power to enforce this article by appropriate legislation.

Section 1. In case of the removal of the President from office or of his death or resignation, the Vice President shall become President.

Section 2. Whenever there is a vacancy in the office of the Vice President, the President shall nominate a Vice President who shall take office upon confirmation by a majority vote of both Houses of Congress.

Section 3. Whenever the President transmits to the President pro tempore of the Senate and the Speaker of the House of Representatives his written declaration that he is unable to discharge the powers and duties of his office, and until he transmits to them a written declaration to the contrary, such powers and duties shall be discharged by the Vice President as Acting President.

Section 4. Whenever the Vice President and a majority of either the principal officers of the executive departments or of such other body as Congress may by law provide, transmit to the President pro tempore of the Senate and the Speaker of the House of Representatives their written declaration that the President is unable to discharge the powers and duties of his office, the Vice President shall immediately assume the powers and duties of the office as Acting President.

Thereafter, when the President transmits to the President pro tempore of the Senate and the Speaker of the House of Representatives his written declaration that no inability exists, he shall resume the powers and duties of his office unless the Vice President and a majority of either the principal officers of the executive department or of such other body as Congress may by law provide, transmit within four days to the President pro tempore of the Senate and the Speaker of the House of Representatives their written declaration that the President is unable to discharge the powers and duties of this office. Thereupon Congress shall decide the issue, assembling within forty-eight hours for that purpose if not in session. If the Congress, within twenty-one days after receipt of the latter written declaration, or, if Congress is not in session, within twenty-one days after Congress is required to assemble, determines by two-thirds vote of both Houses that the President is unable to discharge the powers and duties of his office, the Vice President shall continue to discharge the same as Acting President; otherwise, the President shall resume the powers and duties of his office.

RATIFICATION OF THE CONSTITUTION

The Constitution was adopted by a convention of the States September 17, 1787, and was subsequently ratified by the several States, in the following order, viz:

Delaware, December 7, 1787, yeas, 30 (unanimous).

Pennsylvania, December 12, 1787, yeas, 46; nays, 23.

New Jersey, December 18, 1787, yeas, 38 (unanimous).

Georgia, January 2, 1788, yeas, 26 (unanimous).

Connecticut, January 9, 1788, yeas, 128; nays, 40.

Massachusetts, February 6, 1788, yeas, 187; nays, 168.

Maryland, April 28, 1788, yeas, 63; nays, 11.

South Carolina, May 23, 1788, yeas, 149; nays, 73.

New Hampshire, June 21, 1788, yeas, 57; nays, 46.

Virginia, June 25, 1788, yeas, 89; nays, 79.

New York, July 26, 1788, yeas, 30; nays, 27.

North Carolina, November 21, 1789, yeas, 184; nays, 77.

Rhode Island, May 29, 1790, yeas, 34; nays, 32.

AMENDMENT XXVI

Section 1. The right of citizens of the United States, who are eighteen years of age or older, to vote shall not be denied or abridged by the United States or by any State on account of age.

Section 2. The Congress shall have power to enforce this article by appropriate legislation.

GLOSSARY

Amendment Addition or deletion from a constitution or law; constitutional amendments may be proposed by a two-thirds vote of both houses of Congress or by a convention called by Congress at the request of the legislatures of two-thirds of the states.

Apportionment The allocation of legislative seats; in the House of Representatives legislative seats are allocated based on state populations.

Articles of Confederation The compact made among the 13 original American states to form the basis of their government; officially adopted in 1781 and replaced by the Constitution in 1789.

Bill of Rights The first 10 amendments to the Constitution consisting of a list of the rights a person enjoys that cannot be infringed upon by the government.

Checks and balances Constitutional grant of powers that ensures each of the three branches of government a sufficient role in the actions of the others, so that no one branch may dominate the others.

Delegate A representative of constituents at a legislature or convention.

Due process of law Protection against arbitrary denial of life, liberty, or property, as stated in the Fifth and Fourteenth Amendments.

Elastic clause Clause in the U.S. Constitution that gives Congress power to make all laws "necessary and proper" to carry out government business.

Electoral College The presidential electors from each state who meet following their popular election to cast ballots for president and vice-president. The number of each state's electors is equal to the number of its U.S. representatives and senators.

Ex post facto law A criminal law that is retroactive and that has an adverse effect upon one accused of a crime; a law that makes an act a crime although not a crime when committed.

Writ of habeas corpus A court order directing an official who has a person in custody to bring the prisoner to court and to show the reason for his or her detention.

Impeachment A formal accusation, rendered by the House, that commits an accused civil official to trial by the Senate.

Implied powers Authority possessed by the national government by inference from those powers expressly delegated to it in the Constitution.

Judicial review The power of the courts to declare acts of the legislative and executive branches unconstitutional.

Precedent A court ruling that has bearing upon subsequent legal decisions in similar cases and that judges often rely on in deciding cases.

Ratification A power vested in a legislative body to approve or reject agreements entered into with other states and constitutional amendment proposals.

Separation of powers Constitutional division of power among legislative, executive, and judicial branches.

Unalienable rights Natural rights that cannot be transferred; according to the Constitution these include life, liberty, and the right to own property.

Veto A legislative power vested in a chief executive that grants him the right to return a bill unsigned to the legislative body with reasons for his objections.

SELECTED REFERENCES

A More Perfect Union: The Creation of the United States Constitution. Washington, D.C.: National Archives, 1986.

American Historical Association and American Political Science Association. *This Constitution, Our Enduring Legacy.* Washington, D.C.: Congressional Quarterly, 1986.

Brant, Irving. *The Bill of Rights: Its Origins and Meaning.* Indianapolis: Bobbs–Merrill, 1965.

Burns, James MacGregor, J. W. Peltason, and Thomas E. Cronin. *Government by the People.* Bicentennial Edition. Englewood Cliffs, N.J.: Prentice-Hall, 1987.

Collier, Christopher, and James Lincoln Collier. *Decision in Philadelphia: The Constitutional Convention of 1787.* New York: Random House, 1986.

Edel, Wilbur. *A Constitutional Convention.* New York: Praeger, 1981.

Garraty, John A., ed. *Quarrels That Have Shaped the Constitution.* New York: Harper & Row, 1987.

Morgan, Edmund S. *The Birth of the Republic, 1763–89.* Chicago: University of Chicago Press, 1956.

Morris, Richard B. *The Forging of the Union, 1781–1789.* New York: Harper & Row, 1987.

Peters, William. *A More Perfect Union: The Making of the Constitution.* New York: Crown, 1987.

Ragsdale, Bruce A. *The House of Representatives.* New York: Chelsea House, 1988.

Ritchie, Donald A. *The Senate.* New York: Chelsea House, 1988.

Rossiter, Clinton. *1787, The Grand Convention: The Year that Made a Nation.* New York: Macmillan, 1966.

Rutland, Robert Allen. *The Birth of the Bill of Rights, 1776–1791.* Chapel Hill: University of North Carolina Press, 1962.

INDEX

Donald A. Ritchie is the associate historian of the United States Senate. His publications include *Heritage of Freedom: History of the United States* and *James M. Landis: Dean of the Regulators* as well as *The Senate*, his first Chelsea House book. He holds a Ph.D. from the University of Maryland and has been a lecturer at the University of Maryland and at George Mason University.

Arthur M. Schlesinger, jr., served in the White House as special assistant to Presidents Kennedy and Johnson. He is the author of numerous acclaimed works in American history and has twice been awarded the Pulitzer Prize. He taught history at Harvard College for many years and is currently Albert Schweitzer Professor of the Humanities at the City College of New York.